Communication at Work

A guide to the communication skills needed at work and on training schemes

Alan Jamieson

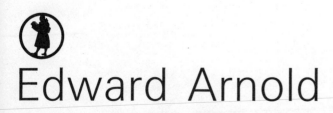

Edward Arnold

First published in Great Britain 1985
by Edward Arnold (Publishers) Ltd
41 Bedford Square
London WC1B 3DQ

Edward Arnold (Australia) Pty Ltd
80 Waverley Road
Caulfield East
Victoria 3145
Australia

British Library Cataloguing in Publication Data

Jamieson, Alan
    Communications at work: a guide to the
    communication skills needed at work and on
    training schemes.
    1. Communication   2. Communication in
    management
    I. Title
    001.51′024658   P90

    ISBN 0-7131-7368-8

Cartoons by Graham Davies (pp 1, 3, 8, 11, 12 and 15) and Rebecca Campbell-Grey.

Text set in 10/11 pt Futura Medium
by Colset Private Limited, Singapore.
Printed at The Bath Press, Avon

Contents

Acknowledgements

The publishers would like to thank the following for permission to include copyright materials:

Michael Heath for his cartoon; Her Majesty's Stationery Office for a graph from Annual Abstract, a Highway Code Sign and an advertisement for the Youth Training Scheme, which are used by permission of the Controller of HMSO; The Automobile Association, British Rail, British Telecom, Lloyds Bank, London Transport and The National Trust for their logos and British Standards Institution for extracts from BS 5378: Part 1: 1980 which are reproduced by permission. (Complete copies can be obtained from BSI at Linford Wood, Milton Keynes MK14 6LE.)

The Publishers wish to thank the following for their permission to reproduce copyright illustrations:

Careers & Occupational Information Centre, Sheffield: p 84; Data General Ltd: p 85, ICL: p 107; Lotus Cars Ltd: p 81.

The publishers would like to state that every attempt has been made to trace the copyright of all material reproduced. We regret any errors or omissions that may inadvertently remain.

Introduction

Communication studies or communication skills are an *essential* part of every City and Guilds, BTEC, and YTS course and of other MSC programmes. For example, the YTS programme isolates these as essential, transferable, skills:

- communication,
- computer literacy,
- manual dexterity,
- number and its applications,
- personal effectiveness.

The major reasons why the MSC has highlighted these skills are because:

- it is felt that young people need to be trained in these skills *before* taking up employment,
- as people will change job several times in their lifetime, *transferable* skills are important.

Communication skills are also part of City and Guilds foundation courses and also apprentice or trainee courses, and they are included as part of CPVE, TVEI and other pre-vocational courses.

This book does not repeat the work done in English classes in secondary schools. It is tied closely to jobs and training, to the skills needed by young people entering YTS or FE courses, or their first real job.

1 Communication skills

When a baby cries for the first time, it is communicating.

From that moment and throughout life, the process goes on. We communicate with each other, first through sounds, then by words and through emotions, and at all times by using our ears, eyes, hands, and other parts of our bodies.

Speaking, listening, looking, reading, writing, drawing, painting — these are among the communication skills. During our years at school, the skills are taught and encouraged. By the time we come to look for a job and to start work, most of us are quite skilful at communicating with people.

Even so, nobody's perfect. For all of us, there is often a big gap between what we want to say and the words we use. And there are many occasions when people misunderstand what they've been told, or mislead others by what they say. Very often, these occasions can be turned into jokes. Here are two: a word joke and visual joke. Notice how the misunderstanding makes them funny.

MEDICAL CENTRE

NOW THEN YOUNG MAN WHATS THE MATTER WITH YOU?

> **Maths teacher:** Smith, if I lay four eggs here, and seven over there, how many eggs will I have altogether?
>
> **Smith:** Well, to tell the truth, sir, I don't think you can do it.

Communication is a link, a connection. When the link is broken, relationships between people break down. You see this in everyday life, when a 'wrong word' causes a quarrel between friends, and when members of a family fail to talk to each other, causing unhappiness and confusion.

This book is about communication at work. It is about some of the writing, listening, speaking, and reading you will be asked to do at work or on a training scheme. The skills you learned at school are important, of course, but once you are in a job or on a training course, you'll be asked to do a different kind of writing. You'll be interviewed — and that involves careful preparation and answers. You'll be asked to read technical books and office instructions — not the kind of reading you did at school, or what you like to read in your spare time.

As you can see, the skills you learned at school have to be applied in a different way. This book has been designed and written to help you to do this: to strengthen the link, the connection, between you and other people at work.

The processes of communicating

The simplest way to explain 'communication' is that it is a *message* passed on from the *sender* to a *receiver* — like this:

This is a simple method of communication, by letter, but the same three parts — sender, message, receiver — are involved if other methods are chosen. Think of newspapers, books, films, radio, television, the telephone — all of them have messages to be passed on to readers, watchers, listeners. But not only do they carry messages — they also have an *effect*. By this we mean that the receiver is influenced, is affected in some way by what he or she reads, sees, hears.

Before we go any further, copy the chart below into your notebook. In the spaces, write the *methods* of carrying the message. Under 'Reading' you could write newspaper, magazine, etc. Under 'Listening' you could put radio, cassette recorder, and so on.

Reading	Writing	Looking	Speaking	Listening

So far, communication looks easy. But, as you know from your own experience, mistakes can happen. Look at the story of Sandra's telephone call. It demonstrates how things can get complicated.

Sandra's phone call

Sandra:	Is that Milton's please?
Receptionist:	Yes, can I help you?
Sandra:	I'm ringing about the job in the paper.
Receptionist:	Who do you want to speak to?
Sandra:	Er . . . I'm not sure. The manager I expect.
Receptionist:	I'll put you through to the personnel manager.
Manager:	Mr Thomas here. Can I help you?

Sandra:	Oh hallo. I'm ringing about the job.
Manager:	Which one? We have several.
Sandra:	The one in the paper. I fancy the office job, I think.
Manager:	Yes, all right. Why are interested in working in an office?
Sandra:	Well, I haven't a job at the moment.

Manager:	Can you tell me a bit about yourself, starting with your name.
Sandra:	Hang on, the money's run out. I'll have to phone back.

Later . . . .

Manager:	Look, Miss, tell me your name and address and if we want to interview you we'll be in touch.

Who is the sender?

Who is the receiver?

What is the message?

It's easy to see who the sender is. But what about the receiver? There are two possibilities. The answer is Mr Thomas, of course — because he's the person who can give information and a decision about a job.

But the message? The trouble is that Sandra made several mistakes. What were they?

In communicating, mistakes often happen because the sender isn't clear and so confuses the receiver. When you make a phone call, for example, you should work out beforehand exactly what you want to say or to find out, so that you get the message clear in your own mind. You should

● ask clearly for the person you want to speak to — the personnel manager, or Mr Thomas if you know him by name;
● give your own name;
● have enough money ready for the phone call;
● explain clearly what job you are interested in.

If Sandra had made a start like this, she wouldn't have confused Mr Thomas.

Response

One of the reasons why communication gets difficult is that there's a fourth part in the sender — message — receiver process. It's called the *response*.

What do you think of this phone conversation?

Jimmy: Hello. Jimmy here. Is that you, Karen?
Karen: Huh?
Jimmy: What about tonight? There's a party over at Malcolm's. Should I call round for you about 8 o'clock?
Karen: I'm never going to speak to you again.
Jimmy: You what?
Karen: You heard. After last night, that's it.
Jimmy: What are you talking about?
Karen: You know. Don't try to be innocent with me.
Jimmy: It is Karen, isn't it?
Karen: No, it's not. It's Janet. You know — that fat, cross-eyed, boozed-up girl you couldn't leave alone last night.

The *response* isn't quite what Jimmy expected. As a result, the phone conversation has gone off in a direction he didn't expect.

Responses make communication difficult. As the message is passed between sender and receiver, new meanings are added, fresh ideas change the nature of the communication. But before we get into this complicated territory, let's analyse some of your communications.

Your messages

Think of six messages you have sent or received today. For each one, list the message, the sender and receiver, and the response. The messages could be, for instance, 'Your breakfast's ready', or 'Fares, please', or 'Ask the storeman for a left-handed brush.'

Let's look at the responses. What was said or done as a result of the six messages?

Most answers are likely to be 'Yes', 'No', 'OK', or something similar. These are common responses. Another kind of response is information given when a question is asked. Here are some questions — think of good responses.

- 'When are you going to get up?'
- 'Where's your Dad gone?'
- 'Will you turn that music down this minute?'

Changing behaviour

Some of the examples in this book ask for (or expect) a change in someone's *behaviour*. This means that the words that are chosen and used (in a letter, on the phone, or in speech) are expected to lead to some kind of action or a change in attitude.

The change can be in various ways:

- by *reaction* (you send a letter and get a reply);
- a change of *decision* (you intended to go to a disco until you were told that Billy would be there, and if there's one person you can't stand it's Billy);
- by changing your *opinion* (as, for example, when you read in the newspaper or hear on the radio a story which makes you mad, wins your sympathy, or in one of many ways leads you to change your mind).

4

Let's look at an example from the world of jobs. Read Paul's story below, and then we'll analyse it.

The new trainee

Paul has been taken on by a manufacturing company as a new trainee.

For the first two weeks, he is shown around the factory — spending some time in the offices, a day or two in the warehouse, a day in each of several sections in the factory, a day out on the road with a delivery man.

In the offices and in the works he sees people using computers, word-processing machines, and electronic control systems. It's all very exciting, and Paul is impressed with what he sees.

At the end of two weeks he's sent to work with Frank, who's been at the factory for several years and who operates one of the big machines which makes cartons.

Frank: What do you think then?
Paul: It's OK. I like it here.
Frank: Any problems?
Paul: Not really. I'd like to do a proper job, like yours, instead of being moved around.
Frank: I've done this job for the past fifteen years, lad. There'll be plenty of time for you to get the hang of it.
Paul: *I'm not going to work on a press for fifteen years. No way!* I want to get on to the computers upstairs, just as soon as I can.
Frank   (sharply): There's nothing wrong with working a press! You don't need to know about computers to work in the machine shop. It'll only take me a day or two to show you what to do, and you're set for life.
Paul: Thanks, Frank. I'd like to know about the press, but I'm going to do the computer course as well. Mr Mason says that part of the training at college will be on computers . . .
Frank: You need brains for that job, lad! If you can work a computer, it'll get you out of the machine shop quick enough. But there are hundreds of us who don't have the brainpower to handle it. Settle for what you can

do, Paul.
Paul: All the same, Frank, I'm going to do the course. You never know, I might understand computing. Anyway, things are going to change in the future. The machine shop won't be here for ever. At this rate, it's not going to last five years, never mind fifteen.
Frank: That's the trouble with the young kids, they know it all. You might be right, lad, but the first thing you've got to do is to learn how to work the press. Now, see this lever here? . . .

Now let's think about Paul and Frank.

1   What's the message that Paul is trying to put across?
2   What's Frank's message?
3   Paul makes a mistake, early on in the conversation. What is it?
4   Will Frank teach Paul the skills of his job?
5   What's Frank's attitude to computers? Is he in favour of them or not?

Think about changing people's *behaviour* or their *opinions*.

6   Would you say that Frank is trying to influence Paul? If so, how does he do it?
7   What's Paul's attitude? Does he give in to Frank, or try to change his attitude?
8   What *action* should Paul take, if any? Should he complain to Mr Mason, or ask if he can be transferred to another operative, or say nothing? Should he go on the computer course or refuse it?

What kind of responses?

By now, you should be beginning to see that communication isn't just the exchange of information. People try to change other's people's behaviour. They try to *influence* them.

Let's look more carefully at different kinds of responses.

Information-giving

This is obvious. People pass on information

all the time through various kinds of communication. For instance:

June: What time do I start?
Manager: Nine o'clock. There's a lunch-break, half past twelve to half past one, and you'll finish at five.

That's easy to understand. All the same, the message has been passed on in a sort of *code*. June has to know what 'half past twelve' and 'five' mean, in order to understand her lunch and finishing times.

In passing on information, therefore, we have to be sure that the receiver understands the code and can 'decode' or 'translate' the message.

What about this conversation?

Frank: What's your name?
Paul: Paul Carlisle.
Frank: Carlisle? That's in Scotland, isn't it?
Paul: No, it's a town in the north of England. But I don't *come* from Carlisle — it's my name.
Frank: They have good beer up there. I once had a holiday in Scotland, but it snowed. And that was in May, too. What did you say your name was?

There's something wrong with this conversation. Frank isn't listening carefully. He's not decoding Paul's message. In fact, he's ignoring it. The word 'Carlisle' has started Frank off on a thinking process all of his own, and he pays no attention to what Paul is saying.

If people give you information, you should acknowledge it with some sort of sign. This is called *feedback* — a form of response.

List three examples of information you have been given recently. Write down your feedback in each case.

Changing people's behaviour and opinions

This has already been mentioned. 'Turn right!' and 'You can't park here, Miss' are expressions which seek to change behaviour. Changing opinions is more subtle, more difficult, but you can see evidence of it every day in *advertising* on television, in newspapers, and elsewhere.

From newspapers, cut out three adverts which are designed to change people's behaviour or opinions.

Another way of changing opinions is by *persuasion*. This may involve some kind of argument or statement backed up by evidence. One of the most important debates now going on is about nuclear weapons. Should nuclear weapons be based in Britain, or does this make war more likely? If so, shouldn't we dismantle all the nuclear-weapon bases and announce to the world that Britain doesn't intend to use nuclear weapons in any future war?

If you follow up these arguments, you will see that both sides (the nuclear disarmers and those who think we should have nuclear weapons) marshall information, ideas, and evidence to support their viewpoint.

Now see if you can do it. Draw up two columns. In the first column put all the arguments for having nuclear weapons, and in the second column put the arguments against having them.

To change opinions by persuasion doesn't need language. People can be influenced by a word, a phrase, a raised fist, a gesture. Then there are insults, sarcasm, mockery, praise, enthusiasm — these all influence our attitudes. What you have to learn is to make *your own judgements* about people and events, and yet be aware that other people might be trying to influence you.

'That's your place, there.'

Putting people in their place is another kind of communication which brings a response. If you think about it, you'll see that people are very sensitive about their position, their place. They can become very angry if others don't recognise their special position — as the boss, the supervisor, the chief clerk, or whatever.

Language, gestures and attitudes are very important in spotting status.

Let's take an example. Chris starts work in an office. On his first day there, he calls the office manager 'Mrs Green'. So far so good — he's been quite formal and has used the polite expression 'Mrs'.

6

But then he hears other people in the office calling her 'Freda'. So on the second day he says 'Good morning, Freda' — and gets a frosty smile in return. Mistake number one: Mrs Green isn't 'Freda' to Chris, only to older people who have known her for some time.

Then the manager comes in. 'Good morning, Chris' he says. Chris decides to play safe this time. 'Good morning, Sir' he replies. The manager turns to him with a smile: 'You don't have to call me "Sir" ', he says, 'Mr Brown will do very well.' Chris can't win!

The third mistake that Chris makes is on the third day in the office. The youngest typist's name is Liz, and she expects everyone to call her Liz. So Chris is all right there. But then he makes a big error. 'Would you like a coffee?' Liz asks him. 'I'm going to get some from the machine.' 'Yes, thanks a lot, darling' says Chris. 'I'm not your darling, nor anyone else's' says Liz sharply. Chris really can't win, can he?

Here are some typical phrases. Thank about them. What *attitudes* would you say are being revealed by the people who use them?

1 'Now then, young man, I'll show you what to do.' (an older worker to a trainee)
2 'Come here, son — quick as you like.' (an order from a supervisor)
3 'What's your name, then?' 'Jimmy Kew.' 'That's a funny one. What do people call you, then — Dole Kew?'
4 'Jimmy, I won't have you calling the headmaster "Belter". He's "Mr Black". Got that?'
5 'Linda, darling, would you be a good girl and type this letter for me before you go home.' (manager to secretary)

Recognising you

People communicate in order to demonstrate their own personality. You can spot (or hear) examples of that every day. Think of the conversations which start up on a train or bus, in shops, and so on.

In doing this, people are responding to a basic human need. They have to establish their own identity, their personality. People hate to be ignored, so they start up a conversation in order to break the ice.

Very often there's a code of spoken language. One of the best-known examples — now a joke — is 'Do you come here often?' as a boy-meets-girl start-up. Another is 'Rotten weather, isn't it?' Can you think of any other ice-breakers?

You'll notice that all these openers or greetings expect a response. 'How are you?' is another popular beginning, and there's the usual coded response to get the conversation going, such as 'Oh, all right, if it wasn't for me legs . . .

So far, all the examples have been of people *talking*. But that's only one form of communication. Responses can also come in written form; in drawings; pictures; gestures such as a nod, a wink, a lift of the hand, a wave, and in many other ways.

One of the ways in which people establish their personality is by their nicknames or appearance. List the names of six people known to you and then alongside write down their nickname (if they have one) or something special about their appearance which makes them different.

Barriers and breakdowns in communication

This book is about *good* communication. But there are barriers to communication, and these cause communication breakdowns. Let's look at some of them.

Barriers

● *Shyness*   There's always someone in the group or on her own who doesn't communicate because she is too shy or withdrawn.
● *Wrong message*   You will have experienced (because everyone does!) the situation where you speak to someone and he gives a reply which shows that he hasn't understood your message.
● *Ignoring you*   Then there's the case when you say something and no one replies. Instead, a different conversation starts up.
● *The wrong words*   In this case your choice of words brings a reaction, a response, that you didn't expect.

Think of some occasions when you have been in the position of finding that there's a barrier to good communication. It could have been caused by shyness, by saying the wrong

thing at the wrong time, by ignoring something which was said to you which you later realised was important, and so on.

Breakdowns

Having seen that there are barriers to communication, let's look at some of the breakdowns which happen.

One excuse for breakdown in communication is often that 'I wasn't told about it.' Another reason is that people don't listen carefully. A third one is people not answering.

Here is a case-study of breakdown in communication in a burger bar. It's based on a real situation.

Chips with everything

Harry's Hamburger Bar was a disaster. The food was good. The service was quick. But the customers were always complaining. And the staff were always quarrelling. In two weeks, five members of staff left, saying they couldn't stand all the squabbling. The managers couldn't understand it — wages were good; profits were satisfactory; staff weren't overworked.

Things got worse. The cooks in the kitchen threw plates on the floor. The servers and waiters were bad-tempered with each other and with the customers. The managers had a flood of complaints from all directions. What was wrong?

A new manager was called in. She saw what was wrong. The waiters and waitresses took the orders from the customers and shouted them through the serving hatch: 'hamburger, chips, and salad'; 'big burger, no coleslaw'; 'double chips on that one'; and so on. The shouted instructions contained all the essential *information* needed by the cooks, and it was a quick way of passing on the orders to the cooks and servers in the kitchen, but the servers and cooks became confused by the number of shouted *instructions*. Worse — the waiters seemed to be giving them *orders*. Who were waiters and waitresses to give them orders!

Miss Goody, the new manager, saw what was going wrong:

- the orders were given too quickly;
- the cooks resented orders being given to them by waiters and servers;
- at rush-times things were worse;
- customers got wrong orders — double chips when they asked for a salad, a

Jumbo when they asked for a Homesteader, and so on.

Miss Goody solved the problem. She worked out a system where the waiters wrote down the order on numbered sheets in a pad. The sheets were put on a spike fixed to a spindle. The servers in the kitchen took the order by turning the spindle; passed it to the cook; and, when the number came up, passed the food through the hatch. 'Number 14' was right: a Monsterburger, green salad, and treble chips. The customer was satisfied.

In the kitchen, too, all was peace. The cooks didn't feel that they were being bossed about by waiters. The servers weren't being shouted at by the cooks or the waiters. And the waiters kept the customers happy.

This chapter has been about what communication is, and what kind of responses result from communication between one person and another. The story of Harry's Hamburger Bar shows how important it is to recognise responses. There was the *required response* (in the case of Harry's Hamburger Bar this was a correct order) and the *actual response* which wasn't the same thing at all.

This teaches us another lesson about communication: that it is a continuous process.

From the simple *sender* — *message* — *receiver* model at the beginning of this chapter, we now move to a model which looks like this:

required response — *sender* — *message* — *receiver* — *real response*

If the responses aren't the same, there's usually a breakdown in communication.

Can you think of occasions when you have experienced some kind of *breakdown* in communication? It could be when you'd had the wrong information, when you misunderstood someone, or when you refused to accept somebody's advice or opinion. Make a list of any *barriers to communication* which have affected you at any time in the past.

2 Why and how

Why

If you went by what you see on the television or in films or read in the newspapers, you'd think that people have four main reasons for communicating:

Asking

People speak out to satisfy their personal needs. This could be in babytalk, or 'What's for dinner, Mum?', or 'Two pints of bitter, John', or in many other ways.

Telling

You'll find plenty of examples of telling. The teacher is one, the supervisor at work is another. Then there's the fortune-teller, or the know-all who has the answer to everything. Newspapers and books come into this category, too.

Selling

Again, you'll be able to spot plenty of examples — shops, adverts on the TV, hoardings, shop-window displays, and so on.

Entertaining

There are the professionals who entertain for a living on TV, in films, and in books. There are people, too, who can't help entertaining you — and themselves — the practical-jokers, funnymen, newspaper columnists, and so on.

But these are just some of the reasons why people communicate. Let's look at these and other reasons in more detail.

1 Personal needs

This is an obvious one. People need work, food, drink, warmth, shelter, love, and other things — and ask for them.

2 Personal relationships

'How are you?' is a starter. People communicate with eyes, hands, words, and gestures to build up a relationship with another person.

3 Information

We all need information of one kind or another. You will be able to think of hundreds of examples. Teachers, doctors, careers advisers, and others spend their lives passing on information.

4 Sharing experiences

This might be telling your friends about your holiday in Cornwall or describing what happened when an idiot driver rammed your Escort. By sharing such information, we satisfy a need to tell other people about experiences which affect us.

5 Persuasion

Advertising is often built on another need — to be liked by other people: think of ads for deodorants, shampoos, soap, and toothpaste. Other advertising concentrates on ambition, desire, greed, and other personal forces.

6 Entertainment

This responds to another human need — to laugh, to be amused, and to share the terrors or tragedies of other people.

7 Learning

Why do people want to learn, to know? It can be because they are interested in a topic and want to find out about it. Or it can be to get on in the world — to find a job, or change it for something better.

Can you think of any other reasons why people communicate with each other? Shown below are seven drawings or extracts from conversations or announcements. Match them to the reasons for communicating listed above — which one is persuading, entertaining, looking for information, and so on?

How

Next, we'll look at *how* people communicate. Here's the start of a list — it's up to you to complete it. Think of as many ways of communicating — sending or receiving messages — as you can and write them down in a list:

● Looking
● Reading
● Writing
● Speaking
● Listening
● Responding

Next, there are many different channels for communicating. Again, make up a list. Here are some suggestions to start you off. Write them down and then add to the list.

● Books
● Films
● Dancing
● Television
● Newspapers
● Singing
● Letters

Both your lists should be much longer then those above.

These methods of communicating can be divided into those which use words and those which do not.

The methods involving words include speaking, writing, and reading and are known as *verbal communication*. 'Verbal' means 'to do with words'.

Methods which do not use words are known as *non-verbal communication*. Advertisers know all about these methods — spot adverts which rely on only a picture to tell the story (there are lots of them about). Cartoonists are another group of non-verbal communicators.

In everyday life, you use non-verbal communication too. Think about how you use your arms, hands, shoulders, eyes, eyebrows, mouth, and nose to express your opinion or to pass on a message. Non-verbal messages can also be passed on through sounds — think of a baby gurgling, crying, laughing, or giggling. And when people do speak, the way they use their voice gives messages to the listener. Do they use their voice softly or loudly? Do they whisper or shout? Do they emphasise certain words? All

these give clues to communication — there's a lot still to find out about!

Here's a breakdown in communication. The fat old lady isn't impressed by the advertisement. Write a new advertisement for the fashion shop, phrasing it so that customers will walk in, not walk away.

A case-study in communication

Having looked at the why and how of communication, let's take a case-study showing the problems of communication within a company. This example shows how important it is to choose the right channel or means of communication, and to know what the message is that you are trying to pass on.

You work for Simon & Sons Ltd, a manufacturing company. You served your apprenticeship there, and then worked for another four years in the production department before you were made a supervisor.

The company changes hands. New owners take over, and a new general manager — Mr Hamfist — arrives. He's full of ideas. One is that people will work much more enthusiastically if they feel they are part of a team. He's right there. But he decides that everyone has to be seen to be equal. He will move his office into an open-plan area on the shop-floor. Everyone — including all the managers — must clock in and clock out. Everyone is to eat in the same canteen — there will no longer be separate canteens for managers and staff. Everyone will take their holiday at the same time, when the factory will close down.

Well, these seem to be good ideas. The staff and the unions all go along with the manager's plans. A few people dislike the new scheme — they feel that hard-earned privileges and rights have been lost — but for the moment they kept quiet.

Next, Mr Hamfist decides on a new plan. In order to improve productivity (that is, produce more goods: this company makes computer parts), everyone will work another hour a day. They'll be paid extra for the hour, at a rate of time-and-a-half. (This means that if they are normally paid £4 an hour, they'll be paid £6 for the extra hour.)

How is he to tell the staff of 108 people? He could do it in several ways. Here are the alternatives:

● a notice, posted on the notice-board;

● a general meeting for everyone (all 108 people);

● a personal notice sent to everyone individually;

● group meetings — about ten meetings at each of which the manager talks to a group of about ten people;

● interview everyone individually.

Mr Hamfist chooses one method and tells the staff. They refuse to have anything to do with the scheme, and the union supports them. No extra hour. No extra pay. Mr Hamfist calls a meeting of the union leaders and threatens them with dismissal if they don't agree to his plan. The union threatens a strike if he goes ahead. In no time at all, the factory, once a happy and contented place, is in an uproar and on the verge of a strike.

What happened?

Well, Mr Hamfist announced his plan by writing a personal letter to all the staff. He explained that recent changes in the company had been successful. However, in order to manufacture more parts, he needed more work from them, both during normal working hours and in the extra hour they were being asked to work. They would be well paid for their work. No jobs would be lost and, with so much unemployment locally, they were lucky to have good jobs which paid well.

It was a very reasonable letter, but it caused a storm. In the end — to cut a long story short — Mr Hamfist had to abandon his plan. Instead, the unions proposed an overtime scheme. People could work extra hours if they wanted to and would be paid overtime rates (also time-and-a-half) if they volunteered.

Could Mr Hamfist have handled it better? Suppose that you were in his position. How would you have handled it? Write down how you would have told the staff (or negotiated with them) for a change in their working conditions.

Now let's look more closely at the different methods of communication.

1   Most communication is *one*-way or *two*-way. If there is only a message from the sender to the receiver its one-way. If there's a reply from the receiver to the sender it's two-way.

A *notice* pinned to a notice-board is one-way communication.

A *personal notice*, sent as a letter to all staff individually, is also one-way communication.

The advantages of one-way communication are that it's quick, efficient, and secure, with everyone being sure to be informed.

The disadvantages are that it doesn't allow for any *feedback* (response) and there's no method of finding out if the receiver has understood the message.

2   Two-way communication allows for questions, discussion, argument. The advantages are accuracy (the receiver can check on what he or she is being told, by asking questions), and the sender can find out straightaway what the receiver's reaction (response) is going to be.

13

Some two-way methods are:

- a *general meeting* for all the staff together;
- *group or section meetings*, with the manager talking to about ten staff;
- separate individual *interviews*.

Mr Hamfist used the one-way system. Did you? He probably thought it would take a long time (and a lot of effort) to talk to everyone individually or in groups. At a full meeting of all staff, he could have been upset by one or two opponents. So he chose to send a *written* message.

You'll have noticed by now that one-way communication is *telling* people, without a response. Two-way communication means a response is expected. It's harder to do, but in the end it's the method more likely to be successful, because people feel that they are involved.

Here are some methods of communication in which you could be involved. Write them down, and alongside each one write whether it is one-way or two-way; whether it is written, spoken, or both; and one advantage and one disadvantage of that method.

- A lecture
- A group discussion
- A telephone conversation
- A letter
- A notice on a notice-board
- An interview for a job
- A film
- A book

Quiz

This quiz tests whether you understand some of the processes of communication and takes you on to the next stage.

1   Which of these picks up *sound* messages?

   a)   Nose
   b)   Ear
   c)   Mouth
   d)   Eye

2   Which of these orders helps you to *concentrate* your mind?

   a)   Stand up!
   b)   Get out!
   c)   Pay attention!
   d)   Jump to it!

3   Which of these is a method of communicating information?

   a)   Computer
   b)   Train
   c)   Bicycle
   d)   Bus

4   Which of these satisfies a human need to *belong*?

   a)   Family
   b)   Food
   c)   Ambition
   d)   Defence

5   Which of these satisfy the need to *do things*?

   a)   Nice clothes
   b)   A job
   c)   A hobby
   d)   Your home

6   Which of these involve communication?

   a)   Making music
   b)   Gardening
   c)   Reading
   d)   Sleeping

7   Do you think people who find it difficult to communicate are

   a)   very shy?
   b)   lonely?
   c)   self-centred?
   d)   bored?

8   Which of these is a two-way process of communication?

   a)   A personal letter
   b)   A telling-off
   c)   A Christmas card
   d)   An interview

The answers

1   The answer to this question is (b) — the ear. All of them pick up messages of one kind or another, but the ear is for sounds.
2   You could say all of them, because they all force you to concentrate on what's being said — a very important aspect of communication — but (c), 'Pay attention!', is perhaps the nearest to the best single answer.
3   The answer is (a), the computer, which deals in numerical and verbal reasoning and information processing.
4   If you think about it, you'll see that people's needs dictate how they communicate and respond. The needs are in several categories (see below) and for this question (a) is nearest to the right answer, because the family involves the need to belong.
5   Another human need is to be able to do things, and so (b) and (c) are both right here.
6   The answer is (a) and (c). Making music and reading are communication processes, but you might also argue that gardening is a communication process too, since it can express someone's artistic feelings, and talking in your sleep could also be a form of communication!
7   Isn't the answer all of them? They all imply barriers to communication.
8   The answer is (d) — the interview. All the others are one-way processes, unless there's a response — a reply letter; a Christmas card hurriedly sent to the sender; an interruption to stop the teller-off from lecturing you.

Understanding the processes

The quiz helped to take us a step further along the road to understanding about communication. Here now is a summary of some of the factors which are important in thinking about how we spend seventy per cent of our time — communicating.

Personality

This football fan is expressing his personality. It's probably the only chance he has of shouting, encouraging, criticising, or celebrating, so he's letting himself go — expressing himself in verbal (and visual) communication.

Concentrating

Question 2 in the quiz was about concentration. The caveman in the cartoon is concentrating too. Your brain is being attacked all the time with information. It

responds by *selecting* some bits of information and rejecting others. So when someone says 'Pay attention at the back!' or 'Watch out — there's a dinosaur behind you!', it helps you to concentrate and to take in what's being said. Failure in communication happens when people don't concentrate.

Understanding

Receiving a message is the first stage — understanding it comes next. Your mind has to *decode* the message. Working from its store of knowledge and experience, your mind decides whether it needs and can understand this new bit of information being thrust into it.

Background

AT WORK, BOYS TALK ABOUT FOOTBALL, SPORT, THE TOP TWENTY, AND GIRLS.

GIRLS TALK ABOUT BOYS, FOOD, WHAT WENT ON AT THE DISCO, CLOTHES.... AND BOYS

You won't agree with what's being said here. At work, people have to talk about their job — what has to be done, how they'll tackle it, what Mrs Smith or Mr Brown said, and so on.

All the same, what people say is affected by their *background*. This means where they live; their family life; what kind of people their parents, family, and friends are; and what kind of opinions they've already formed. For instance, if you think boys *only* talk about football, you'll probably start up a conversation with 'Weren't City a load of rubbish on Saturday?'

Motivation

This word — motivation — means what drives people. It could be ambition, it could

be promotion, it could be money. In communicating, motivation is very important. The reason for this is that people respond much more quickly if they think that what they are being told will help them towards their objective — a job, a Rolls Royce, a holiday in Tunisia, or whatever motivates them at the moment.

Needs

In the quiz, there were two questions (4 and 5) on needs. Here's a list of some of the important needs which drive people to communicate:

a) survival — food, drink, shelter;
b) security — a home, defence against attackers;
c) belonging — the family, friends, marriage, children;
d) approval by others — this means the need to feel that you are seen in a good light by your family, friends, and workmates;
e) self-fulfilment — this is the need to do things, to follow up your own abilities, to create, to 'do'.

The situation you are in at any one moment decides the priority of these needs. Starving people in Africa would put food highest on their list. In Britain, a good job would be an important priority.

Where are you?

Now let's turn to you. It's time to stop and think about all the things we have discussed in relation to your life, your job, your interests.

1 Make a list of the things which *motivate* you. (Another way of putting it is to say 'what turns you on'.) Among them could be money, a good job, children, and so on.
2 Then, from this list, make a list of priorities, 1 being the most important, 2 the next most important, and so on.
3 Next, make out another list, headed 'Work'. What are the factors which you think are important at work? When you've made out your list, put the items in order of priority too.
4 Put yourself in this position: Littlewoods has come up! You've just won £100 000

on the football pools. What would you do? Start your own business? Travel around the world? Give up studying? Start studying for a new career?

5 If the company you worked for insisted that you had to move to another part of the country, what would you say: yes or no? If you say yes, and move away, what would you miss most — your home, family, friends; your town; your job; or what?

6 What *needs* do you have? Write them out in order of their priority.

3 Looking

Using your eyes is one of the most important of the communication skills. You might think first of 'giving someone the eye', in the sense where 'boy meets girl'. That's one kind of eye-to-eye contact, and it can be very effective.

At work, however, looking is important too. It is essential to look carefully at tasks that are being set; to look at people who are explaining things to you; to look at notices, instructions, letters, and other written forms of communication.

Let's start by setting you some tests.

In this drawing, there are four children's faces. Can you find them?

The next test is to look at the parts of a television:

Now look at the half-completed television below. Cover up the finished television and complete the drawing in your workbook.

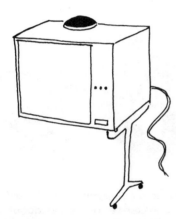

Compare the two drawings. What differences can you see now?

Looking is important for good communication because:

- you have to *concentrate*;
- although it's a one-way process, if there's a response it becomes *two*-way communication;
- it aids motivation;
- you have to be *accurate*.

Can you think of other reasons why looking is so important?

Now let's go on to examine these skills in more detail.

Observation

Observation means looking at something very carefully, and learning from it. You'll find out that at work you can learn a lot from watching how people do things. If you copy the good examples, and apply them, you'll be doing yourself a good turn. If you copy the bad ones, then you'll soon be in trouble.

Let's take some examples. Here's how Linda dressed up for an interview for a job in an office. She's smartly dressed, neat, and clean. Is this an example to follow or not? What do you think?

Sally got the job. Here she is at her desk. Why do you think Sally was successful and Linda wasn't?

What would you wear if you were going for an interview for a job:

a) on a building site?
b) with a rock group?
c) at a big store such as Marks & Spencer?
d) in a garage?

Would it make any difference what you wore?

Signs, posters and notices

Signs

How good are you at recognising and following signs? Let's start off with another test. What do these signs mean?

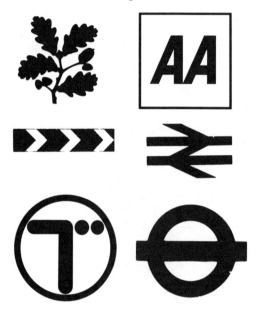

Once a sign becomes accepted, it is part of everyday life. Road signs have to be learned by heart and by eye, of course, so they can be instantly acted on. Companies like to promote their products with a sign (usually called a *logo*) which people know — this is very effective advertising. Can you think of the logo or sign for these companies: Penguin Books, British Leyland, British Home Stores? Draw them and three other logos.

Posters

Another way of catching people's attention (that is, communicating an idea or a product to them) is by means of posters. Again, if you use your eyes, you'll spot posters which make a strong visual impact. What would you say makes posters such as Guinness advertisements so effective?

Design and draw a poster. It has to 'sell' something — you can decide what — beer, toothpaste, a car, or, better still, a product of the company where you work or where you've spent a period of work experience.

You should make your poster especially eye-catching. But remember it has to carry a message, which is usually 'Buy this'. The poster is the message between you — the company manufacturing or selling the product — and the receiver, the customer.

Notices

At work, you will come across all kinds of notices. They tell you about safety precautions such as fire escapes, emergency exits, and so on. You will be told to read notices about safety rules on machines, the danger from slippery or oily floors, dangerous stairs, and so on.

On the main company notice-board, there could be another set of notices about meal times, sports or social-club events, training schemes, holiday dates, or union meetings.

On the next page is a selection of notices seen in a factory. What do you think of them? Are they effective? Do they get the message across?

The next time that you are in a factory or offices, look at the notice-board. Which notices catch your eye and hold your attention? Is it because you notice the headline and it immediately sparks your interest? Is it a subject such as sport or the next disco which you are keen on? Or is it

Diagrams

You'll find out that an essential part of many jobs is following and drawing diagrams. These can help a great deal in communication. For instance, if you are trying to explain to a friend how to reach your home, you could say, 'Look, I'll draw a map.' That's a kind of diagram. Another kind is a diagram which shows you how something works — a toaster, record-player, washing-machine, and so on. At work, you'll have to cope with all kinds of diagrams such as factory plans, assembly instructions, computer charts, and so on. So let's have some practice in following and drawing them.

the notice itself — well-designed, eye-catching, direct, and to the point?

Select one of the subjects given below (or choose a different topic which interests you) and design and write a notice about it.

- A sports meeting or outing,
- The canteen menu for today,
- Danger!
- Join the union!

The way to the top

Here's a diagram which shows the structure of a company. Not *all* companies are organised like this, but many are similar to it. Notice that Alice and Andy are starting at the bottom.

Let's suppose that Alice has her sights on being the managing director. Follow her path to the top!

Andy is in a different department. Which one is it? If he's going to make it to the top, he has to obtain qualifications and

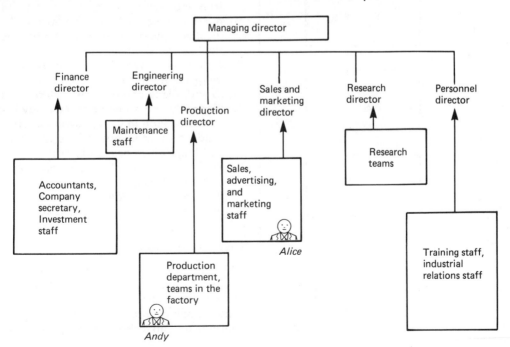

experience in production work. What kind of work would Alice specialise in?

'From the way the diagram is drawn, would you say that it's easy to make a switch in this company from one department or kind of work to another? Suppose Andy wanted to cross over from production work to finance: what new line could be drawn to show the route he might take?

Teamwork

Betty and Billy aren't yet ready to move into the managing director's chair. They are both part of a production team of fifty people in a factory. The map below shows the layout of the assembly shop. There are four main processes before the goods are sent to the warehouse. The numbers of people working in the sections are shown in the boxes.

You should be able to work out how the system operates.

1 If there are fifty people in the team, how many managers and supervisors are there?
2 The production team are supplied by parts which come on trolleys. You can see three of them in the drawing. Can you think of a more efficient system of moving the parts from one section to another?
3 Notice where the manager's and the supervisor's offices are built. Are they in the best place to control production? What changes would you make?
4 Betty works in the wiring-and-soldering section. She tells the supervisor that there's a safety problem. What could it be?

Now it's your turn

1 The manager in the shop where you work tells you that the customers can't find their way to the electricity department. She asks you to draw a diagram which will be pinned up at the shop entrance.

    The electricity department is on the first floor, reached by a flight of stairs from the back of the ground floor. The main entrance (where the notice will be displayed) is at the front of the ground floor of the shop.
2 On another sheet of paper, draw a diagram of the route you take from home to your place of work, the college, or a place which is some distance away from home. Include in your drawing all the roads, footpaths, bus stops and major buildings which are landmarks.
3 You've been asked to draw your ideal car or house. Design it, marking on your drawing the outstanding features — style, safety, and so on.

Instruction books

At work, you'll often have to use instruction books which give you a step-by-step introduction to a work-task.

Each book or manual probably has a list of contents and an index. The contents tell you

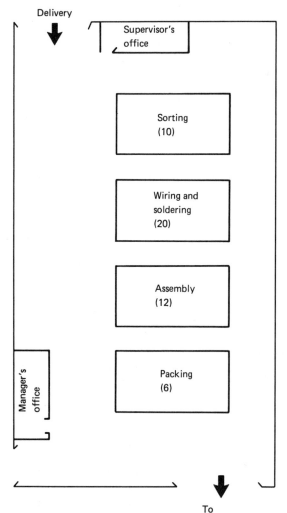

Delivery

Supervisor's office

Sorting (10)

Wiring and soldering (20)

Assembly (12)

Packing (6)

Manager's office

To Warehouse

where to look for help with some particular aspect of the machine. The index has the page references to special parts of the machine or a special skill.

A coffee-maker

Look at the drawing of the coffee-maker.

1 Find where you put the coffee. Do you fill the coffee basket to the top?
2 Which part of the coffee pot shows the water level required?
3 What do you think these are:

   a) the well?
   b) the spreader plate?

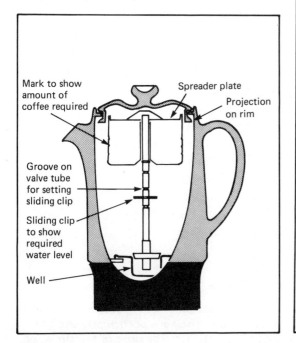

Mark to show amount of coffee required

Spreader plate

Projection on rim

Groove on valve tube for setting sliding clip

Sliding clip to show required water level

Well

Plugging-in

Here's another diagram, and a set of instructions. Study the diagram and information and answer the questions.

1 What colour is the live wire?
2 Which wire is connected to N?
3 Suppose you are using the appliance with a 13 amp plug. What fuse would you need?
4 What colour is the earth wire?
5 Suppose you had an old plug with the terminals marked Red, Black, and Green. Which wires would you connect to

   a) Red?

How to connect a plug

WARNING

THIS APPLIANCE MUST BE EARTHED AND IS SUITABLE FOR USE ON AC SUPPLY ONLY

Check that your supply corresponds to that shown on the rating plate. The appliance must only be used from a 13A or a 15A power socket. If a BS 1363 13A plug is used it should be fitted with a 3A fuse. If in doubt consult a qualified electrician.

IMPORTANT The wires in this mains lead are coloured in accordance with the following code:

GREEN-AND-YELLOW : EARTH
BLUE   : NEUTRAL
BROWN   : LIVE

As the colours of the wires in the mains lead of this appliance may not correspond with the coloured markings identifying the terminals in your plug, proceed as follows:
The wire which is coloured GREEN-AND-YELLOW must be connected to the terminal in the plug which is marked with the letter E or by the earth symbol ⏚ or coloured GREEN or GREEN-AND-YELLOW. The wire which is coloured BLUE must be connected to the terminal which is marked with the letter N or coloured BLACK. The wire which is coloured BROWN must be connected to the terminal which is marked with the letter L or coloured RED.

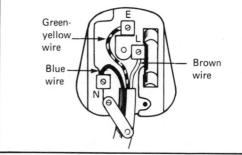

Green-yellow wire

Blue wire

Brown wire

b) Black?
c) Green?

Now you

Borrow a car instruction manual and use the list of contents to find the instrument panel. On the diagram of the panel, find these:

a) the speedometer,
b) the brake warning lamp,
c) the heater control,
d) the fuel gauge,
e) the sidelight switch,
f) the ignition switch,
g) the direction-indicator switch.

23

Use the index to find the engine. Find out where these are:

a) the engine number,
b) the engine oil dipstick,
ç) the oil pump,
d) the starting plugs,
e) the distributor.

Graphs

Another way of demonstrating quite complicated information is by means of charts. These can be graphs, bar charts, maps, or other forms of display. One kind of chart is a graph. The graph below shows the growth in population in England and Wales during this century. The dotted line shows the estimated population in 1966, which was about forty-eight millions.

Find out:

a) the population in 1901, 1921, 1951, 1981;
b) the estimated population in 1945 and 1975.

Population of England and Wales, 1901–1981

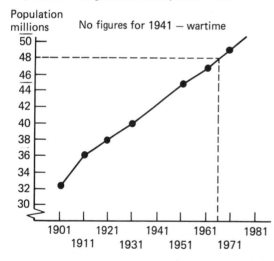

Bar charts

Bar charts are another way of presenting information (they are not a guide to how much you can drink in a bar in one night!)

A bar chart consists of blocks or bars whose areas are proportional to the numbers being presented. It cannot be absolutely accurate, but it is effective in comparing similar things. Let's look at an example.

Smartypants Ltd

This company has a successful export record. Last year, it sold 400 000 pairs of its famous 'Smartypants' for export. The bar chart shows the overseas countries which bought the pants and the approximate number sold in each one. Can you read it?

1 What was the biggest export market?
2 How many were sold to each of Canada, France, and Ireland?

Smartypants

'000s sold

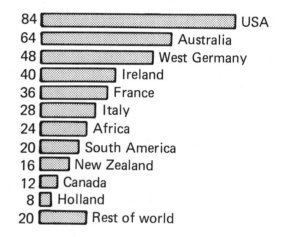

Pie charts

Pie charts are an effective way of presenting information. They are particularly useful for showing statistics. The area of the circle, or pie, represents the total amount of the sum involved. The size of each slice is then proportional to the value of the part it represents. A pie chart can show, simply and clearly, the proportions of different parts.

The pie chart opposite shows the proportions and the figures when a thousand people were interviewed. They were asked 'What daily newspaper do you read', and the slices of the pie show how many people read each newspaper.

a) What were the three *most* popular newspapers, in order of their popularity?
b) What were the three *least* popular newspapers?

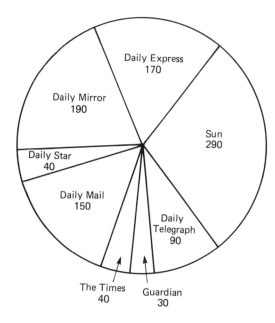

Daily Express
170

Daily Mirror
190

Daily Star
40

Daily Mail
150

Sun
290

Daily Telegraph
90

The Times
40

Guardian
30

Now you try

In one year, Perfect Printers Ltd made its money from these sources of income: book printing, £20 000; magazines, £30 000; stationery, £10 000; government contract printing, £20 000; export contracts, £12 000. Draw a pie chart to illustrate this information.

Picture-stories

Another way of communicating ideas and information visually is by picture-stories. The word usually used to describe these diagrams is 'pictogram'.

In pictograms, we can use symbols instead of words. The usual way of doing it is to make one symbol (such as a person's head) represent, say, 10 000 people.

Let's look at an example. The illustration below shows (by means of coffins) the causes

Cause of death	
Heart and circulatory diseases	1901 ⬭⬭⬭⬭⬭⬭⬭ 1981 ⬭⬭⬭⬭⬭⬭⬭⬭⬭⬭⬭⬭⬭⬭⬭⬭ ⬭⬭⬭⬭⬭⬭⬭⬭⬭⬭⬭
Cancer	1901 ⬭⬭⬭⬭ 1981 ⬭⬭⬭⬭⬭⬭⬭⬭⬭⬭⬭⬭
Infectious diseases TB fevers	1901 ⬭⬭⬭⬭⬭⬭⬭⬭⬭⬭⬭ 1981 ⬭

of death by certain diseases in England and Wales. What do you notice about these figures? Is the symbol effective?

What symbols would you use to show

- hospital beds?
- TV sets in houses?
- unemployed people?
- employed people?
- people in prisons?

Draw a pictogram to illustrate the following annual output figures for a vehicle manufacturer: saloon cars, 100 000; lorries, 20 000; sports cars, 30 000; buses, 10 000; motor cycles, 5000; ambulances, 4000.

Plans and maps

Another way of presenting information is by means of plans and maps. We shall look at two examples.

Fast Services Ltd

The map below shows the main rail and road links used by Fast Services Ltd.

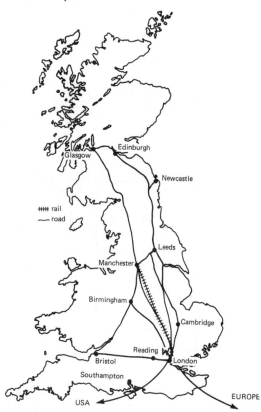

Glasgow
Edinburgh
Newcastle
⊞⊞ rail
— road
Leeds
Manchester
Birmingham
Cambridge
Reading
London
Bristol
Southampton
USA
EUROPE

The company has decided to make its headquarters and main distribution centre at Watford (marked W on the map). The main road and rail links are shown on the map.

1   Is Watford a good centre? What are

    a) its advantages?
    b) its disadvantages?

2   Fast Services does most of its deliveries by road and rail. Is Watford in a good or a bad position for deliveries *overseas*?
3   Suppose you are the managing director. Where would you choose to put the distribution centre, assuming you have a free choice?

The map question above was set as part of a test for people applying for a job with a company. The plan and the questions on it below were also set as part of an entry test.

The company, an engineering works, wanted to see if trainees could read and analyse a layout diagram. Now you try.

Fuzzy Engineering Ltd

The layout shows an assembly shop at the works. The problem was that, as the taps and mixers came in from the polishing shop on a conveyor, problems interfered with the smooth running of the assembly shop. Can you spot the problems and work out the solution?

1   There are two groups of 'goods'. What are they?
2   With your finger, trace the routes taken by the mixers and the taps.
3   What do you think about the position of the supervisor's office?
4   What are the main problems with this layout?

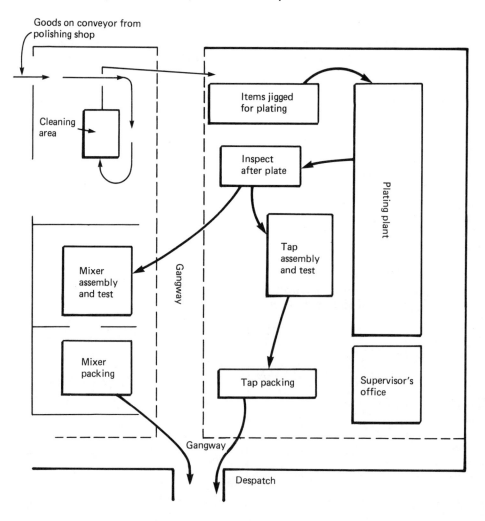

26

Keep looking — and surviving

This chapter has been about *looking* — about using your eyes to spot information and about using visual symbols or drawings to record or transfer information.

These skills are very important in a job. You'll find lots of diagrams and drawings which you're expected to follow. This means reading or studying them carefully, and obeying the instructions exactly. One of the most important ways of using these skills is in following safety instructions.

Safety at work is something which will be stressed time and again. The reason is obvious — you'll be taking great risks if you don't observe safety rules. And you could be making it dangerous for your friends and workmates, as well as for yourself.

How many people each year do you think are killed at work in the UK: is it 10, 50, 500? The answer is about 900 people each year are killed in industrial accidents — and thousands more are injured.

On any one day, how many people in the UK do you think are away from work because of an accident or injury suffered at work — 100, 1000, 10 000? Again, the answer is more than you might expect: about 60 000 people *on any one day*.

Let's therefore put the 'looking' skills to practical use.

1   Walk around the factory, store, offices, garage, college, or other place where you are working or studying. As you go round, draw a plan of the place. On your plan, show where these are: exits, fire alarms, fire blankets, first-aid boxes, fire extinguishers.

2   Next, from the management or safety representative (every place of work has a safety officer or safety representative), find out how many accidents occurred over the last twelve months. Draw a pictogram or a bar chart to show the causes of the accidents — burns, falls, collisions, moving machinery, or whatever.

3   Finally, walk around again. This time look for potential (possible) safety dangers. Draw a plan of the area and on it show where these hazards (dangers) are.

4 Speaking

Most communication is by *speaking*, whether it is at work or when you are with friends or at home.

If you think about it, you will realise that speaking skills involve these factors:

- the *words* — what you say, that is the choice of words and how they are grouped in a phrase or sentence, is very important.
- the *voice* — the tone of the voice gives a clue to the meaning of the words. The voice can be used loudly or softly, to warn or to encourage, and in many other ways.
- the *tone* — everyone knows that the way we say something gives a clue to the speaker's meaning. Try saying 'Come here' in several different ways or tones of voice (firmly, softly, fiercely, and so on) and you'll see what we mean.

Look at the cartoon opposite. What you have to do is imagine what might be said — and *how* — by four people. What do you think would be said by

a) the election candidate?
b) Mrs Voter?
c) her husband?
d) the baby?

Speaking at work

A trainee, a student, or a young employee has to learn quickly how to speak to people. This means choosing the right words — and choosing the right way to say them.

The best advice is to speak clearly, watching the other person (the receiver) to see what kind of reaction there is. Does the receiver look bored, puzzled, astonished, angry? If the response is 'Eh, what's that? Would you say that again?', you know the message isn't getting through.

To demonstrate this, say a word or a

phrase such as 'Would you come here, please?' in different tones of voice, as if you were giving an order, offering an invitation, asking someone (politely) to do something, dealing with a difficult customer, and replying to an instruction from your boss. When you've done this, you'll realise how important it is to use your voice to get the reaction you want.

Now try this. Here are some common phrases. Say them out loud. Then say the same phrase again, using a different tone of voice. You could be polite, firm, sarcastic, or use any tone you choose.

- Watch out there!
- Excuse me — would you mind moving over here, please?

- Where have you been?
- Shut that door!
- Pass me the hammer!

Accents

Employers expect people to speak clearly. They are far more interested in clear speaking than in the accents people have. Regional accents are quite acceptable. It would be a very boring world if everyone spoke in the same way with the same accent.

However, an accent may be so strong that people from outside its area can't understand what is being said. In that case, the accent should be toned down. It might be difficult to sell shoes in Bristol with a thick Geordie accent — there'd be more chance of selling the Bristol folk some coal than a pair of wellies!

Numbered 1 to 9 are some approximations to phrases that are quite common in some parts of Britain. Say these phrases out loud. They would be quite acceptable at a workplace in their area, because people there would know the meaning of these phrases. But if you were answering the phone and speaking to someone living two hundred miles away, you might tone down the accent. At the other extreme, you wouldn't use the phrases lettered A to I, although they mean the same as the regional phrases above them. Can you match them up? When you've done that, what would *you* say in these circumstances?

1 Gizzit heor, man.
2 Summat oop wi'thee, lass?
3 Ee's cum ower funny.
4 Gorrah lite, mite?
5 Ow'd un? Ee's oot back.
6 Sit thee doan, lad, an't wait a minnut.
7 Orl royt, guv'nor, oi'l be dahn in a sec.
8 Aah divven knaa a thing aboot it, aah tek wor lass doon the toon.
9 Ah, Jimmy, ye ken the we'ans, they're awfu' poorly.

A The foreman is attending to it at the rear of the premises.
B Don't be perturbed, sir, I shall be down in a moment.
C Are you not feeling well, Miss?
D James, do you know, I believe the children are unwell.
E Please hand it to me.
F Do you have a light, please?
G Please sit down, sir, I shall be with you in a short while.
H He is feeling faint.
I I know nothing of this since my wife and I were in town.

Standard English

An employer won't expect you to use 'standard' or 'BBC' English. By this we mean the kind of voice that BBC newsreaders have. The reason why broadcasters speak in this way is so that they can be understood in any part of Britain. Even so, many BBC and ITV announcers have quite pronounced regional accents. However, the same rule applies to them as it should to you — they speak *clearly*.

Using your voice

The way in which you speak is very important. For example, if you speak in an aggressive way, people will react angrily or defensively. If a customer says, 'Can I change this sweater, please?' and you scowl and reply, 'We don't usually exchange goods once they've left the shop, but just this once I'll change it', it is unlikely that the customer will ever come back to your shop. The way you speak is also important at an interview, for if you answer the interviewer in a slow bored voice you'll soon be shown the door.

Speaking up

Young people who are in their first job have to be careful about what they say and how they say it. They have to learn quickly how to judge the words they use and the tone of voice they think is appropriate.

For example, it's not always the best idea to be the first to speak — let the supervisor or an older employee have the first word (and the last word, too). If you talk too much, you'll soon be put in your place. You'll know how people feel about you when they pick on a nickname. If your workmates call you 'Bigmouth' or 'the Gaffer', you'll know it's time to shut up.

On the other hand, you are expected to have an opinion and, if you are silent, other

nicknames will be aimed at you such as 'Chatty' or 'Gabby' ('he's got the gift of the gab') or 'the Squeaker' (a joke about Mr Speaker, the chairman in the House of Commons). These names show another way of using the voice — through sarcasm. You should be prepared, therefore, to speak up when you feel you have something to say.

Speaking skills

Let's make a list of some of the speaking skills you may need at work:

- answering the telephone,
- dealing with customers,
- talking about the job with the training officer,
- putting your viewpoint at a union meeting.

Next, think of two people you know — call them Able and Glum. Mr or Ms Able is very good at speaking. Mr or Ms Glum is a poor speaker. Now, what are the qualities that make Able good and Glum poor? Make a list of the two sets of qualities: Able is a good speaker because . . ., and Glum is a poor speaker because . . . .

Your list of speaking skills should include these suggestions:

- *Speak clearly*   To be a good speaker, you need to be able to put your ideas across very clearly. Your language should be simple and direct. Your material — words and ideas — should be well organised. Don't use long complicated words and sentences if simpler ones will do. And, as well as *thinking clearly*, it's essential to *speak clearly*, too. This means saying the words distinctly, so that they are easily recognised.

- *Speak accurately*   You also have to make sure that the words *say what you mean.* Facts should be correct, so make sure that you know what you are talking about.

- *Be friendly*   You should be polite and friendly. If you feel angry, you should control your emotions. The use of your voice and the expression on your face are both important here.

An activity which will help you to understand and develop your own speaking skills requires a tape or cassette recorder. What you have to do is this:

1   Read a section of a newspaper out loud and record your voice on the recorder.
2   Make a second recording, this time with a friend. Record a conversation. What did you notice about your voice on the playback? Was there any difference from the first recording, when you read from a newspaper?
3   Read from a document you've been given at work — an order, a safety instruction, etc.
4   Record yourself at work, speaking to your boss or to a senior member of the company.

What differences can you detect between the first two recordings and the last two? It is possible that you may sound awkward or frozen when talking at work. What you should do is to make more recordings at home, practising the use of your voice, breathing deeply, and relaxing. If you do this, you'll find that your speaking skills quickly improve.

Body language

Body language is the way we use our eyes, hands, and the rest of our body to help with communication. Study the cartoon. Look at these things in the drawing:

a)   how the two men are dressed;
b)   their eyes;
c)   the expressions on their faces;
d)   the use made of the rest of their body — the hands, shoulders, head;
e)   what they are saying.

The cartoon tells us a lot. It helps us to understand body language.

The eyes have it

Eye contact helps you to appear friendly — or aggressive as in the cartoon. Have you talked to people who never look you in the eye, who look at the sky, over your shoulder, out of the window? How did you feel about it? It's likely that you became bored with them very quickly. Learn the lesson then: when you are speaking, keep looking at the receiver. Catch his or her eye regularly, smiling as you do so. It helps a lot in putting the message over.

Looks are important, too

How you look — your appearance — also

affects how well people understand you. The way you look is a sign of how you see yourself — your self-image. People form opinions about other people even before they have spoken. They do this by making judgements on the evidence of the clothes they wear and their general appearance. This means neatness and cleanliness. It doesn't mean we all have to dress alike. What it does mean is that whatever clothes are worn for work — a suit, overalls, jeans etc. — must be neat and clean.

Standing and sitting

These are part of body language too. If someone is leaning against a wall or slouching at a desk when speaking to you, with head drooping, it gives a very bad impression. In any case, if you drop your head or let your shoulders fall, it affects your breathing — your voice sounds muffled and indistinct. Try it and see. The general impression can be of a slow, hangdog, confused person — someone who wheezes or whines as he or she speaks.

Instead, you should give the impression of alertness, briskness. This is done by sitting straight, standing up with the shoulders back. If you try this, you'll see that your voice comes out more briskly, more clearly — and that's what impresses people.

Gestures

People emphasise what they are saying by gestures. Look at the interviewer in the cartoon. Notice his raised fist. People emphasise what they are saying by waving their hands, shrugging their shoulders, winking, shaking their head, and in many other ways. Gestures are an important aspect of speaking skills — they show the emotion, the feeling, behind what's being said.

There are subtle ways of using your body, too. Simply not moving is one. At school, you will have seen how teachers can become very annoyed by the silent (or 'dumb') insolence of a pupil. That's a technique to avoid. Mr Smithers didn't use it. His insolence is verbal — in the language he uses in his reply — and in the expression on his face.

Being yourself

It would be a mistake to think that we all have to be the same — be polite at all times, dress alike, speak alike. Whatever you do, you must not crush your personality, your individuality. This book isn't for yes-men and yes-women. People get jobs and then move on within them because they *use* their personalities. That's what this book is all about — how to make the best use of your personality.

Another objective is to show you how to avoid mistakes in communicating and, in this chapter, with speaking. One way of doing this is to observe other people. Keep your eyes and ears open at work. Notice how people speak; how they gesture; how they use their hands, eyes, and the rest of their body, including the voice. Put these observations into two groups — those which *help* communication and those which *hinder* it.

You decide

Look at the following three drawings. In your notebook, under these headings, describe the ways in which the three people are communicating through:

a) speech,
b) the way they are dressed,
c) body language.

THE DHSS? YOU WHAT.....?
NEVER MIND THAT, I'VE GOT
A COMPLAINT TO MAKE.
NOW JUST LISTEN....

EXCUSE ME, I'M FROM THE TAX OFFICE. I HAVE AN URGENT PROBLEM TO DISCUSS WITH THE MANAGING DIRECTOR.

HARD WORK NEVER HURT ANYONE. LOOK WHAT IT'S DONE FOR ME, SANDRA.

Using the telephone

Being able to use the telephone is an important asset for any job. It sounds easy, but there's a lot of skill involved in it.

You have already seen (in Chapter 1) how *not* to use the phone. Now let's use the speaking skills you have learned to improve your telephone techniques.

For young people going into a job or a training scheme for the first time, there are two main purposes in using the phone:

- telephoning for a job or an interview;
- using the telephone as part of the job, such as answering a customer's inquiry or ringing up a supplier.

Let's take each one in turn.

Telephoning for a job

We shall suppose that you've seen an interesting job advertised in a newspaper. It says 'Telephone 235478 for further information.'

If you are phoning from a public call-box, you have to make careful preparations:

- Have some change ready to feed the coin-box.

- Have a pencil and paper handy, so you can write down essential information given over the phone (such as the place and time of an interview).
- Write down the name of the person you want to speak to (if it is in the advert) and the job title if there is one (e.g. 'trainee office worker').
- Think of two or three questions about the job. Write them down, so you can refer to them during the phone call.
- Have your personal description (your 'c.v.' — see page 68) ready, so you can answer questions about your qualifications, work experience, etc.

Practice

Using the phone is just like learning to ride a bike — you become better at it the more practice you have. At the start, you are likely to be nervous. And, if you follow the advice given above, there will seem to be a lot to remember and a lot of things to do at the same time. But if you practise these skills, you should find that your confidence grows.

You won't get this practice by telephoning for job after job. That would waste other people's time as well as your own. But you could use your tape or cassette recorder. With a friend taking the part of the employer, you could practise telephone calls. To start you off, here are two job advertisements. Using the recorder and a friend as your 'stooge', telephone the company or organisation, asking for more information and answering the interviewer's questions.

County Council, Department of Housing. Ref: 34/JL Young person needed to train as clerk in busy office. Phone Mrs Liz Cox at 242 4563

Good opportunities for school leavers to earn more than £50 p.w. with expanding manufacturing company. Hours 8 a.m. to 5 p.m. Monday to Thursday, 8 a.m. to 1 p.m. on Fridays. Training given. Phone Factory Manager, Useful Products Ltd., 782 3567.

Finding out by phone

Another use of the phone is at work, perhaps dealing with customers, or with other companies, repair and maintenance people, and so on.

How do you deal with a situation where your boss says, 'Phone them and find out about . . .'? Here's how Lynn did it. Did she make any mistakes?

Telephoning a customer

There are some general rules to follow when telephoning a customer. Lynn made one or two mistakes, didn't she?

Here are some hints, in a step-by-step sequence:

- When you get through, say 'Good morning' or 'Good afternoon.'
- Give your name and your company's name.
- Say the name of the person you want to speak to. If you don't know the person's name, say to the operator or receptionist 'I'd like to speak to someone about ordering . . .' whatever it is.
- If you are cut off, replace the receiver, wait a few seconds, and try again, saying to the operator 'I was trying to get Mr So-and-so, but was cut off.'
- When you are passed to the manager, you might say 'Hello, is that Mr Whatsit? I'm phoning with an order . . .', explaining why you are contacting him.
- Again, give your name and your company.
- Mr Whatsit might want to say something. Pause for a moment, giving him the chance to speak. If you have done your preparation correctly, you'll have a pencil and paper at the ready to take down details, such as a name and address, order number, etc.
- Spell out anything that might be difficult to understand, such as a name.
- At the end, confirm the order or any action required or a date to be met. Like this: 'Very well, Mr Whatsit. I'll arrange a meeting of the finance committee for ten o'clock on Tuesday 13 March.'
- If you have to leave a message, be brief and keep to the point. Don't ramble. Tell the person at the other end what to write down: 'Would you please ask Mr Smith to phone me between four o'clock and five o'clock today?'
- At the end, thank the person you are speaking to for helping you. Even if you didn't get an order or the information you want, you still want to make a good impression, so say 'Thank you for your help'.
- It is usual for the *caller* to end a conversation (on the grounds that he or she is paying for the call), but you may

have to give a gentle hint: 'Yes, I've taken a note of the times, Mr Whatsit. I'll tell the manager the moment he gets in. Thank you.'

When the call is over, complete your notes so you can understand them later. Put any dates in your diary or the manager's diary. Pass the results of the call to anyone who needs to know the information.

Notes should be brief but contain the essential information. Here are three. Two are correct. One isn't much good. Which is the dud one?

1   'Your car won't be ready today. Telephone the garage manager, Mr Toms, at four p.m. tomorrow.'
2   'A Mrs Somebody rang from Swintons. It's all fixed.'
3   'Phone John Stanton at 021-421 5326 before two o'clock. He wants to know when the radiators will be ready.'

Talking on the telephone

'Hello. Is that Cheapjack Tours?'
   'Yes. Jack Knowall, the manager, speaking.'
   'Right, then. My boss wants a ticket.'
   'At your service. Tell me: where to, when, and by what method — air, sea, rail, road, or cycle?'
   'You what? Oh, I see. Well, er . . . she's going to Glasgow for a sales meeting. I think she wants to go by air. Or is it by train? Hang on, I'll ask her.'

Clearly, the caller is very confused. The essential information hasn't been prepared. The manager is brisk and knows his business, but his cleverness confuses the caller.

What you have to do is to write out the questions that the caller probably needs to ask, such as train or aeroplane times, dates, prices, how to collect tickets, and so on. Write these in one column. In a second column, write the answers which the manager would be likely to give.

Find out about company telephones

If you know of a company, or if you have worked for one on a work-experience or similar kind of project, find out

a) the company or organisation's telephone number;
b) how its telephone system works (it could be a school or college system, with extensions, just like a company);
c) if calls come through an operator;
d) how an incoming call is transferred;
e) how outgoing calls are logged or registered — do people ask the company operator, dial a special number, or use some other method?

5 Listening and interviewing

Listening is neglected — sometimes ignored — as a communication skill. But, if you think about it, you'll realise that you spend a great deal of your time listening to what people say to you. When you do the listening, it can be face-to-face, on the telephone, in lessons and lectures, or through radio and television. If you add listening to music to the list, listening occupies a major part of your time.

While preparing this book, a survey was made of twenty young people who were in a job and attending college on a day-release course for one day a week. First of all, it was discovered that in each hour of waking time, they spent forty minutes communicating in one way or another. Then, analysing *how* they communicate, the survey's results came out as shown in the pie chart below. What do you notice? The important fact is that they spent a lot of their time *listening*. (Sleeping time doesn't count!) For each hour, they

spent five minutes writing, seven minutes reading, and so on. Notice the time they spent *listening*.

Listening skills

At school, everyone is taught to read and write. But it is very rare for anyone to be taught *listening skills*, unless there is a physical hearing problem.

The only kind of advice most people come across is 'Listen, you lot! I've something important to tell you!' At home, it's quite likely that your mother or father will say 'Do you *ever* listen to anything I say?'

It is often assumed — wrongly — that, because people have ears, they don't need to be taught to listen. Although to some extent they learn to listen by instinct — by watching people's faces, hearing their tone of voice,

How the hour was used

LISTENING

WRITING

5 minutes

READING

7 minutes

18 minutes

10 minutes

20 minutes

SPEAKING

NOT COMMUNICATING

'HEY! WATCH OUT, THERE!'

DID SOMEBODY SAY SOMETHING?

following the ups and downs of the words, picking up the message through their ears — there are still skills which can be taught.

Another aspect of listening is *forgetfulness*. Research has shown that most people forget *half* of what they were told within five minutes of hearing it! Five days later, they can remember only twenty per cent of what they heard. So listening has a high failure rate, even though we spend most of our time doing it! That's why people often say to you, 'Hang on, I'll just write that down' — they know instinctively that they are likely to forget what they have been told, so they reach for a pen and paper.

Listening at work

In a job, listening skills are very important, as the victim in the cartoon on the previous page is about to find out.

As a trainee on a company training programme or in your first job, you'll have to do a lot of listening. Words will come at you from all directions.

First, there are your friends and workmates, who will want to talk about their problems. Then there's the training officer or your supervisor, whose job it is to tell you about aspects of the job you will be doing. Then there are the twenty or so people who work alongside you, who will know far better than the supervisor how things should be done and will want to tell you about it.

Next there is the training you'll get at college. This means listening to lecturers and tutors, trying to follow what they are saying about new subjects that you'll be studying.

All this adds up to a lot of listening — and people will expect you to retain what you hear. They will say 'I told you about that yesterday' — expecting you to remember what you were told, despite the other information flung at you since then.

This means that you should try to be a 'good listener'. Let's find out what that means.

Good listening

At work, it's a big advantage to be a good listener. This means concentrating on what is being said, remembering as much as you can, and then acting on what you've been told. If you don't do this — that is, if you become a bad listener — you won't learn the job, you won't follow instructions properly, and you won't make progress in your work.

Here, then, are some reasons why it's important to improve your listening skills:

● to get to work or college on time,
● to understand the information given to you about your job,
● to be able to follow instructions properly,
● to be able to reply to people who ask you questions,
● to improve your relationships with other people.

Understanding people

Listening carefully to what people say helps you to understand them. But it does something else, too — it improves your relationship with them. If you pay attention, and show by your attitude that you are concentrating on what they are saying, they are likely to be a lot more friendly and co-operative. On the other hand, if you don't attend, look away, or fool about, you will annoy the speaker and lose his or her help.

Look at the drawing opposite. The supervisor is explaining something about the job. He is looking directly at the three trainees. Would you say that the three are listening? What about the girl? Her eyes are fixed on the supervisor and her manner shows that she is concentrating. But there is something about her attitude which shows that perhaps she is too relaxed, that she may not be fully concentrating. What is it?

And what of the two young men? What do you notice about their attitude? Give reasons why you think they are good or bad listeners.

Are you a good listener?

How can you be trained to be a good listener? Before we answer that one, here's a test to see how good you are already.

1 Do you look directly at a speaker while he or she is talking to you?
2 Do you break into a conversation whenever there is a pause?
3 Do you keep your mind on the topic of the conversation?

4 Do you ignore what the speaker is wearing and pay attention to what is being said?
5 Do you not always insist on having the last word?
6 Do you place yourself in a room so you can hear clearly what's being said?
7 Do you listen to the tone of the speaker's voice, so that you can judge the emotions or feelings which lie behind the words?
8 Do you consider the other person's point of view, even though it might not agree with yours?

If you scored eight 'yes' answers, you can go straight on to the next chapter because you are perfect — an excellent listener!

On the other hand, if you answered 'yes' around five times, you aren't perfect but it sounds as if you are honest with yourself.

Think again about your 'no' answers — they provide clues to why you aren't a good listener. It may be that you 'switch off' when people talk about something that doesn't interest you. Or you may be more interested in the clothes they are wearing or their hairstyles than in what's being said.

The eight questions above are a good guide to listening problems. Once you recognise what these problems are, you should find it easier to improve your listening skills.

Aids to listening

Here is a list of ten 'aids to listening'. These are aids to help you to be more effective, more efficient, as a listener. Write down which ones are very important for you, which ones you need to practise, and which ones could be useful to you.

● Concentrate on what's being said.
● Avoid distractions such as looking at the speaker's clothes.
● Pick out the main ideas.
● Be interested.
● Look directly at the speaker.
● Think how you could use the information.
● Even if you don't agree with what the speaker says, don't be put off.

- Weigh up in your own mind the usefulness or value of the information.
- Don't interrupt the speaker.
- Afterwards, make notes of the points which you want to remember.

Body language for listeners

In the previous chapter you read about body language — that is, how the eyes, hands, arms, and other parts of the body help people to express themselves.

The way that people sit, stand, and use their head and limbs help with listening skills, too. For instance, if someone you are talking to gazes out of the window, slumps in a chair, or falls asleep, you might get the impression that he or she doesn't find your conversation very interesting.

Good listeners don't look up at the ceiling, or yawn, or sigh — they look directly at the speaker, perhaps nodding in agreement or shaking their head, smiling, and in other ways showing that they are following the drift of the conversation. They are *sympathetic* to the speaker. They are encouraging and helpful, and these attitudes may lead the speaker to think that he or she is talking to a friend, an ally. At work — as at home or anywhere else — a person who is sympathetic and encouraging in this way is likely to be popular. This skill is, for instance, one of the keys to the success of a salesperson.

Activities to help you to be a better listener

1 If you have a cassette recorder, record ten minutes of a radio programme you enjoy. Listen to the recording. When it is finished, wait a few minutes and then write out the main points of the programme. This is a good way to test your concentration.

2 If you are in a group of young people on a training course, at college, or at school, take it in turns to stand up and tell the rest of the group about yourself. The information could include your name, address, spare-time interests and activities, holidays, and so on. Another member of the group should take notes.

3 During the course of a day, watch the body language of listeners. Make lists of the things people do. One list might be negative actions such as yawning, looking out of the window, slouching in a chair. Another list could be positive things such as nodding, saying 'Yes, of course' or 'What happened next?', and using the head, arms, and body to show that the listener is concentrating on what's being said and is helping the speaker.

Being interviewed

One situation in which speaking and listening skills come together is in being interviewed.

One kind of interview which everyone knows about is a *job interview* — but there are others, too. When leaving school and going to college, there is an interview with a lecturer. When joining a training scheme, there are interviews with training officers, careers officers, and managers. Then, once you are in a job, there are interviews with the supervisor, the manager, the trade-union shop-steward, and so on. Some of these will be formal, where you answer questions put to you by two or three interviewers; others will be informal, where someone will say, 'Come on, we'll have a chat about it . . .', but in their way these are interviews too.

Preparing for an interview

If you apply for a job, change your job, or attend an interview for one of several reasons, there's usually a form to be filled in which asks for personal information — your full name, address, education, qualifications, work experience, and so on. Interviewers base their questions on what you write on this form. It is very important, therefore, to have all this information summarised so you can quickly refer to it. In Chapters 7 and 8 of this book, on writing techniques, you'll find out how to do this. In this chapter we are concentrating on what is *said* at an interview.

Going on

'You can go in now', says the receptionist. We'll assume that you've been through all the preliminaries. You've completed the application form, dressed neatly, and found your way to the receptionist. Now you are on your own, faced by a panel who are going to judge whether or not you are good enough or suitable for the job, the place at college, or the promotion.

You knock on the door. A voice says 'Come in.' You go in. If the interviewer says 'Do sit down, please', avoid sitting in his or her chair. Watch how the interviewer sits. If it is in an upright, alert position in a chair, do the

same. It's the first clue to body language. Don't plunge down into your chair as if you'd run all the way from the station.

Wait until you are spoken to.

If the interviewer nervously lights a cigarette, don't do likewise. Suppose you are in front of three interviewers and one of them lights a cigarette and then offers you one. What do you do? The answer is whether you smoke or not, say 'No, thank you — other members of the panel might be non-smokers, and you could annoy them.

Questions, questions, questions

You are now settled comfortably, ready for the first questions. These could be 'starters' such as 'Did you have any problems getting here?' What you mustn't do is to launch into a long story about how the bus was late, you had a flat tyre, etc. You should give a quick and precise answer, and then wait for the next question.

As the questions are asked, don't fidget. Keep looking at the interviewer, answering calmly and accurately.

To give a good impression, there are some general rules to follow. Below are some interview 'Do's'. Below those are some 'Don'ts'.

Do

- sit straight in your chair,
- listen carefully to what's being said,
- keep your eyes on the interviewer,
- keep your hands still,
- sit still,
- be polite and friendly when you speak.

Don't

- cross and uncross your legs,
- gaze out of the window or at the ceiling,
- swing backwards and forwards in your chair,
- clench your fists, twiddle your fingers, pick your nose, wave your hands,
- argue with the interviewer.

Change places

One of the keys to being well prepared for an interview is to put yourself in the interviewer's place. Then you have to think about the questions you would put to a victim. Let's do that.

Suppose you were interviewing someone for a job. What is important? Below is a list of things. As an interviewer, which do you think are important and which not important?

- arrives punctually
- has punk hairstyle
- looks strong
- is relaxed in manner
- keeps cool
- is bright and alert
- is serious
- laughs a lot
- argues his or her case
- wears matching clothes
- is good looking
- looks you in the eye
- wears jeans
- can't keep still
- asks questions
- is shy
- uses long words
- has a c.v. (personal record sheet) handy

What do you say?

You should now realise that it pays you to think out what you are going to say *before* you go to an interview.

There are questions which are bound to be asked — about your school, qualifications, spare-time interests, work experience, and so on. You should have rehearsed the answers to these questions in your own mind. Better still, you could practise being interviewed, with a friend or parent acting as the interviewer. If you record a practice interview, you should be able to spot the listening and interviewing skills which are important for you.

Avoid one-word replies. The worst answers are 'Yes' and 'No' — they tell the interviewer very little. Think out answers which are two or three sentences in length.

There is one skill which will take you a little time to learn. It is an important part of listening and of replying. This is to give an answer in such a way that it leads the interviewer to ask you another question, and one which shows off your good points. Here is an example:

'Can you tell me what you've done since you left school, Alice.'

'I went on a training scheme and then I got a job in an office.'

'An office? That sounds interesting. What kind of office.'

'Well, my friend's Mum started a little business, altering and selling clothes. I did the office part of it, answering the phone, a bit of typing, talking to customers, . . .'

Alice has managed to turn the conversation so that she can tell the story to her advantage.

Let's think a bit more about answers to 'leading' questions. (These are questions which are designed to lead you into making a positive response.) Here are ten questions that are often asked at job interviews. If you were asked them, what would be your answers?

1 Did you like school? What did you like best about it?
2 What were your best subjects at school?
3 What do you do in your spare time?
4 Are you any good at maths or English?
5 Have you had any part-time jobs or work experience?
6 Why did you apply for this job?
7 Do you know what we make (or do) here?
8 Would you like to go on a training course here or at college?
9 What makes you think you'll enjoy working here?
10 Are there any questions you want to ask?

Have you any questions?

You should always have one or two questions ready, just in case an interviewer says to you, 'Do you want to ask about anything?' At a job interview, you could ask about:

- wages,
- holidays,
- the kind of work you'd have to do,
- training,
- weekend work,
- canteen meals,
- who you'd be working with,
- college courses.

At an interview, people can easily make mistakes by asking long questions and by asking too many questions. If the interviewer glances at the clock, you know it's time for you to go!

In the three drawings below, the three people being interviewed have each made a mistake. What mistakes have they made?

I KNOW THE INTERVIEW IS AT TEN, SQUIRE, BUT I THOUGHT I'D BE EARLY.

JOB CENTRE

THE JOB I WANT NEEDS TO BE WELL PAID, OUT IN THE OPEN, AND NO OVERTIME

FACTORY ENTRANCE

ME DAD SAYS IF I DON'T GET A JOB HERE, HE'LL HAVE THE FACTORY OUT ON STRIKE

Group interviews

It's possible that when you are called for an interview there are two, three, or more people there. Instead of being interviewed on your own, you may be part of a group. In this situation, it's even more important to listen carefully and to be good at communication skills. The reason is that you may be in competition with the others.

Many people find this a difficult situation, and dry up. They are too shy or unnerved to say anything. But you shouldn't be put off. You have to understand why some companies have group interviews. It's usually to see how people behave when they have to work together, or when they come up against rivals.

What should you do? Interviewers are looking for people who are sensible and can work easily with other people. In this case, you must be natural and straightforward. You mustn't sulk or stay silent — all you are doing then is proving that you can't work with others.

Listening . . . and speaking

Interviews are a match of careful listening and careful speaking. But, as you can see, other communication skills are involved, too. Writing is important, for you won't get to an interview unless your letter of application and the c.v. (the personal record sheet) are correctly written. Reading plays its part, for interviewers will expect you to have read about the firm or the organisation before you attend the interview.

Job interviews are only one kind of interview. Think of others — at school, at college, at the doctor's. Each of them involves all the skills mentioned above, but most of all listening and speaking. And all of them involve *questions*.

Interviewers have a lot of experience and know how to phrase questions to make it easy or hard for people to answer them. Sometimes the question can be a *direct* one, such as

- 'Have you had a job?'
- 'Can you type?'
- 'What CSEs have you got?'

Or, the question can be *open*, giving you the chance to offer a longer answer, and so make a good impression:

- at college: 'Can you tell me about yourself — your interests, for example?'
- at the Jobcentre: 'What kind of work would you like to do, Mr Milne?'
- at work: 'What do you think you've learned here in the last six months, Margaret?'

Then there are *probing* questions. These get below the skin, make you think, make you respond:

- 'What would you say are your best points, Michael? And your worst?'
- 'In the time you've been here, Mary, what do you think you've achieved?'

'*If you were*' questions aren't easy either:

- 'If you were the manager here, what improvements or changes would you make?'

Lastly, there are the *check-up* questions. Tony says to the interviewer 'I'm very interested in cars', and the man on the other side of the desk says 'Oh, I see. Well, . . . could you explain what a carburettor is for?'

Activities

1 Draw a series of cartoon pictures to show someone attending an interview. Most of the things he or she does are right, but in the cartoons you have to add one mistake made by the interviewee. Ask a friend to spot your deliberate mistake.
2 Practise some interviews with other people in your class or group. One of you can be the employer, the personnel manager, or the welfare officer. When you finish the interview, change round and change the subject. The more interviews you can practise, the better you will get at the important communication skills of listening and talking.

6 Reading and finding out

People who have spent the last eleven or twelve years in school don't want to be told how to read! By the age of sixteen, most people have got the hang of it.

On the other hand, there are many people who for one reason or another don't master the skill of reading. For them there are special adult literacy classes where they can get expert help. And there are students from overseas who have difficulty with English because it is a strange and foreign language to them — they too need special classes.

At the age of sixteen, seventeen, and older, therefore, we should be able to assume *some* reading skill. What has to be developed then are methods of *improving* people's ability, so that they get a lot more out of reading for pleasure, or for work, or for knowledge. This means spending time to improve reading skills, to be able to read faster, read technical handbooks, read for understanding, and read to learn.

Let us start by making a list of the reasons *why* you need to improve you reading skills:

- for pleasure (a book, a music magazine, a newspaper);
- for information (what's on at the cinema, bus and train times, the football results);
- for safety (road signs, notices in the factory or office);
- for a job (job adverts, an application form);
- as part of your training (manuals, notices, college books);
- in your job (instruction sheets, pay-slips, union rules).

Can you think of any other reasons? Write them down, adding examples in brackets, as above.

Finding out

You will have noticed that some of the reading skills you need are linked closely to *finding out* about things. In your job, in training, and at college, there is a lot to be found out. This means searching through reference books and textbooks, using newspapers, consulting technical magazines, and so on. This is why we have linked *reading* with *finding out*. It is essential to be able to read quickly, carefully, and with understanding if you are going to be able to find out about things in order to do your job effectively.

Reading and finding-out centres

You could say that there are three main kinds of place where you can practise reading and finding-out skills. They are

- *skill centre:* this could be your local college or school, or a special adult literacy centre (where they give help to adults who find it difficult to read), or an evening class;
- *information centre:* the library, a bookshop, a company's reading room, a newsagent's shop — these are all places where you can obtain information;
- *advisory centre:* this is anywhere that provides special help or information — a Jobcentre, a reference library, the Citizen's Advice Bureau office, the health centre.

Each of these places — and many more — provides a special kind of service. In some of them (such as a college classroom) you can improve your reading skills. In others (the library) you can find and read the information you need.

A ONE-MAN INFORMATION CENTRE

200	Religion
300	Politics and social sciences
400	Languages
500	Pure science
600	Technology and applied science
700	The arts
800	Literature
900	Geography and history

Indexes

In each of the sections in a library using the Dewey system, there are likely to be hundreds — perhaps thousands — of books. The sections are therefore subdivided. For example, electrical engineering is in the 620s, and books on Africa are at 960.

In order to find your way to the book you need, you should look at the library's *subject index*. This gives you the Dewey number for books on the particular subject.

If you know the writer's name, look in the *author index*. This is arranged by surname, just like the telephone directory. The index will tell you the Dewey number so you can go straight to the right section.

For practice, find some books and their Dewey numbers. In your local or college library, find out the Dewey number for books on these topics and write down the titles and authors' names of two books on each subject:

- careers,
- farming,
- sports,
- do-it-yourself,
- nursing,
- computers.

The third kind of index you should use is the *book index*. Let's suppose you have found the book you want on, say, aircraft. But it's helicopters that you really want to find out about. Turn to the back of the book, where you should find the index, and look for 'helicopters'. If there isn't an index at the back, check the table of contents at the front of the book.

In the reference library

A reference library usually contains special books such as dictionaries, encyclopaedias, guidebooks, local history and geography,

Books

Books are only one resource for reading, but they are the main resource. In your work, you will find that time and again you will be told to 'Get a book on it', 'Look up the reference', 'Bring me the facts.'

There are plenty of books about using the library, on 'how to study', and so on. Ask your tutor or your local library about these. Here, we are concerned about directing you to the main sources of information — after that, you will have to ask for advice from the librarian.

Most libraries have four main sections:

- the lending library (fiction and non-fiction books),
- the children's section,
- the reference library,
- the reading room (for daily newspapers and magazines).

Within these sections, most libraries arrange books on shelves according to the Dewey system, which is a decimal reference system. Books are placed in ten main categories:

000	General books
100	Philosophy and psychology

road maps, travel guides, music scores, medical books, telephone directories, and car manuals.

Most of these books are heavyweights. It's likely that you'll need to use only one of them. Use the index to find the topic you want.

Here is a list of books you should find in a reference library. Match the books to the descriptions in the list below.

1 *Kelly's street directory*
2 *The Oxford dictionary of quotations*
3 *Who's who*
4 *The children's encyclopaedia*
5 *Whitaker's Almanack*
6 *Ranking and Spicer's company law*
7 *Keesing's contemporary archives*
8 *The careers encyclopaedia*

A *Facts and figures about the world*
B *Famous people*
C *Information about jobs*
D *A new chapter a week is added to a book on the latest events in the world*
E *A guide for businesses*
F *An A-to-Z book of information useful for pupils in school*
G *Names and addresses of people living in your town*
H *Famous literary sayings and who wrote them*

Reading at work

The next stage is to apply your reading and finding-out skills to work. First of all, what *special* reading skills do you think are needed for training, in doing a job, to understand business life? The answer is that there are no *extra* reading skills. What are required are *practice and care* with the skills you already possess.

In reading, for example, you won't have to read everything at the same slow pace. Sometimes you'll need to read quickly when you are searching for a particular bit of information. Sometimes you will have to go more slowly in order to follow and understand a complicated piece of writing. Let's look at some examples.

Test your speed

Here is a table of reading speeds. You can test your own reading speed by reading two or three pages of a book, making sure you understand what is written there. Time yourself as you read. Read for five minutes, then count up how many words there were in the pages you read in those five minutes and work out how many words you read per minute. What was your score?

Reading speeds (words per minute)

0—50	very slow
50—100	slow
100—150	average
150—250	fast
250—400	very fast
400 and over	genius speed!

Careful reading

There are other times when reading slowly and carefully is very important. For example, if you have to follow wiring instructions for an electrical installation or a plug. Or if you have to follow the step-by-step instructions in a technical manual. In this case you must go slowly, perhaps going over the same sentences several times until you have remembered or applied the information.

Let's take an example. On the next page is an extract from a book about computers. Read the extract slowly and carefully and then answer the questions without checking back to the text. When you have written the answers, check them for accuracy.

Notice that the description of the computer is written in short, clear sentences. The writer knows that a computer is a complex piece of machinery, so the language is kept simple, to help the reader's understanding.

The computer

There are various kinds of computer. However, they all have the same basic layout.

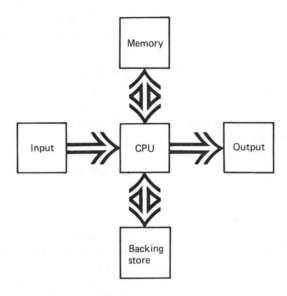

The *CPU* is the central processing unit. This is the brain of the computer. It deals with all the calculations and it controls all the different parts of the computer.

The *memory* stores the information. The ability to store large amounts of information in a tiny place is a powerful feature of any computer. To use the brain, you have to put information into the computer and take out of it the results of the calculations. Input to the CPU is through the keyboard. The computer-user types his or her instructions through the keyboard. *Output* from the computer goes on to a screen or VDU. The VDU is the visual display unit which has a screen similar to a television screen. Another output is by means of a printer, if a permanent copy is needed.

The CPU contains very complex electronic circuitry. It is divided into two sections. One part does the calculations: this is the ALU or arithmetic logic unit. The second part of the CPU controls the whole computer, including the memory, the ALU, and the input and output devices. This is called the *control unit.*

One of the most important parts of the computer is the memory. The memory is used to store the program and the information on which the program works.

A *program* is a list of instructions. The computer has to be told what to do and how to do it. The program is made up of instructions telling the computer what job has to be done. The control unit in the computer reads the program (which is then stored in the memory) and carries out the instructions. The control unit does this by sending signals to different parts of the computer.

The *backing store* is used to store programs and data (information) for later use. The backing store is a quick way of recording programs and playing them back into the computer when they are needed. The backing store uses two devices: disk and tape. When a program is needed from the backing store, the computer-user releases a command from the keyboard on the input device. The computer loads the program into the memory from the backing store. The computer-user then asks for the program to be run.

Test your reading

1 Is a CPU the memory, the output, or the brain of the computer?
2 One kind of output is on a printer. What other kind of output is there?
3 One part of the CPU controls the whole computer. What does the other part control?
4 How are instructions passed by the computer-user to the CPU?
5 What are the two devices used by the backing store?

Skimming and scanning

Obviously, in order to understand how a computer works, you have to read the information slowly. But there are other occasions when you need to read fast. Two methods of doing it are by 'skimming' and 'scanning'.

The idea of skimming is to go quickly through a book or a leaflet, noting in your head (or on a piece of paper if, unlike a computer, you can't trust your memory) the vital pieces of information you need — 'See Chapter 4, pages 78—90' etc. Then, having found out where the important bits are, you can return later for careful reading.

Skimming is also rather like drawing a sketch-map. Your mind registers the outline, the coastline. Later, you'll put in the rivers and cities — that is, the detailed information.

Scanning is rather different. It means looking through a book for a particular piece of information. You need scanning skills when you are using an encyclopaedia, a telephone directory, a technical manual. When you run your eyes down a list, an index, or a job sheet, you are scanning for the item of information you need.

Selecting

Another reading skill is selecting. This is useful when you are 'finding out', that is looking for information in reference books. With practice (and you need plenty of it) you will be able to spot the main points of a book or a chapter, selecting the bits you require.

Here is a test to see how quickly you can select. Below are a list of job titles and a list of descriptions of what's involved in the jobs.

Select three job titles. How quickly can you match them to the right job descriptions? Time yourself.

Job titles

1 Coal miner
2 Nurse
3 Bank clerk
4 Market-gardener
5 Hairdresser
6 Library assistant
7 Typist
8 Clothing machinist
9 Postman
10 Car worker
11 Railwayman
12 Plumber
13 Painter

Job descriptions

A Knows about books.
B Calculates and handles accounts.
C Uses a keyboard.
D Works underground in a team.
E Handles cloth.
F Takes care of people who are ill.
G Grows flowers and vegetables.
H Has to know where roads and houses are.
I Prepares surfaces for decoration.
J Learns about cutting and styling.
K Finds out how an engine works.
L Answers passengers' enquiries.
M Learns about water systems.

Read that, will you, John?

Let's take some more examples of the kind of reading you may have to do at work.

Everyone feels nervous about starting work. This is quite natural, for everything is new and strange. There are new routines to be learned, and no teachers to check on whether you have learned them or not.

Before you start work, the company or organisation will probably send you a letter, setting out starting times, breaks, finishing times, and other details of the job. This letter is a test of slow and careful reading — not one for scanning or skimming.

When you start, there may be a clocking-in system. If so, you'll be told about it. Next, you have to find out who's the boss. There may be several bosses as far as you are concerned — the manager, the supervisor, the training officer. They may all give you things to read — safety instructions, terms of your contract, job orders, and so on. These have to be read very carefully, too.

Next, someone may say, 'There's a training course here. You'll find the details in the office, John. Get a copy and find out what you have to do, and when.' That is the first 'finding-out' job you may have to tackle — finding your way to the office, discovering where you have to be and at what time for training or college attendance, and so on.

Contract of employment

A contract of employment is a document (it could be a letter) which explains the terms offered to you and which you accept. An employee (says the law) must be given a contract of employment no later than thirteen weeks after starting work. The contract gives information on pay, weekly hours, training, overtime rates, and other details.

Here's another reading test.

Below is a list of things which have to be included in a written statement which forms the contract of employment. Read the fourteen points. Then turn the page over and write down the fourteen points from memory. How many did you get right?

- The date on which you started work
- The employer's name
- The rate of pay and how it is calculated
- Whether payment is weekly or monthly
- The weekly hours of work
- Overtime timings and rates
- How much holiday you get and the rate of holiday pay
- Starting and finishing times
- How much notice you have to give before you leave
- How much notice they have to give you before dismissing you
- Sick-pay details
- Pension arrangements

- The company rules about discipline
- The name of the person you can complain to if there's a problem about work

Reading your pay-slip

A pay-slip is something which people read very carefully indeed. The reason is that, obviously, it states the money they have earned. But another reason is that the slip is often in a kind of code, which has to be deciphered.

Some people are paid weekly; some are paid monthly. There are other workers, who work on a temporary basis, who are paid daily.

You will probably get your pay in a special envelope. Some companies arrange for pay cheques to be paid into bank accounts, others give Girocheques which can be cashed at post offices.

Whatever the method of payment, you'll be given a pay-slip explaining what you have earned and listing the deductions taken from your pay. Opposite is an example of a pay-slip. Not all are like this one, but it includes most of the deductions that are likely to affect you.

What does it mean?

Match the explanations given here with the words or phrases on the pay slip.

A   Payment advice
B   National Insurance number
C   Company number
D   Tax coding
E   Gross pay
F   Special additions
G   Taxable pay to date
H   Tax
I   Pension
J   Union dues
K   Total deductions
L   Net pay

1   The amount agreed by the company with the union to be deducted monthly for union membership
2   In large companies every member of staff has a number
3   Bonuses, overtime payments, etc.
4   The actual take-home pay
5   The name for the pay-slip

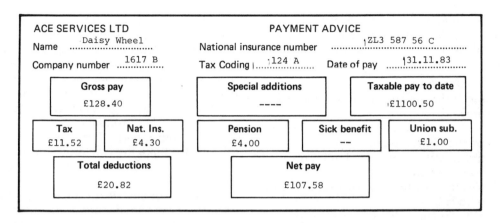

ACE SERVICES LTD		PAYMENT ADVICE		
Name: Daisy Wheel		National insurance number: ZL3 587 56 C		
Company number: 1617 B		Tax Coding: 124 A	Date of pay: 31.11.83	

Gross pay		Special additions	Taxable pay to date	
£128.40		----	£1100.50	

Tax	Nat. Ins.	Pension	Sick benefit	Union sub.
£11.52	£4.30	£4.00	--	£1.00

Total deductions	Net pay
£20.82	£107.58

6 Deductions towards the company's pension scheme
7 The total pay before any deductions
8 A tax number showing the code which is the rate at which you pay tax
9 All the deductions added together
10 Your individual number within the state insurance scheme
11 The amount of tax paid this month
12 The amount earned since the start of the financial year (beginning of April)

Reading for information

Most of us read to obtain information. When you pick up a newspaper, it's usually to find out the news of the day. If you want to know about something, you'll look for a book or a leaflet about the subject.

At work, you will find that information is presented in different ways. In the first place, there are books, booklets, loose-leaf sheets, and so on. You will also come across information given in drawings, diagrams, maps, charts, plans, and tables. You will be expected to understand these *visual* methods of presenting information, that is to be able to *read* a diagram or table.

Let's take an example. The diagram below shows the structure of Big Boy Manufacturing Company. Just think how many sentences and words would have to be used to explain

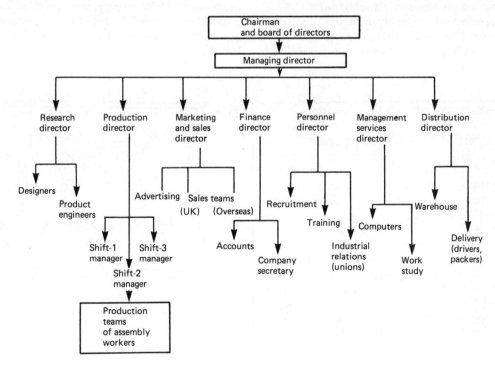

this structure. A diagram does the job simply and clearly. But can you read it? After you've studied the diagram, answer the questions below.

1 Excluding the chairman and managing director, how many other directors are there?
2 Which director would you say is likely to have the biggest workforce?
3 Which director is responsible for new product design?
4 Which director handles negotiations with the trade unions?
5 Which director is likely to be in charge of the company's publicity and press releases?
6 What would you say are likely to be the main duties of the management-services director?
7 If you wanted a job with this company, which department would you approach?

Reading with understanding

We have already explained that you must *understand* what you read. If you don't understand, you won't remember what you've read. It would be a waste of effort.

That's a bit obvious. *Reading with understanding* is slightly different, and not so obvious. This means that we must train ourselves to read information very carefully,

to sort out and sift the facts, and to think about them before making up our minds.

If you read carefully, thinking about the real meaning which lies behind what you read, you'll have a better chance of seeing the truth, of not being 'taken in' by the writer. Again, let's look at an example.

Sandra and Mick read the notice below. 'Dodgy!', said Sandra, 'There are one or two things I don't like the look of.' 'It sounds great to me', said Mick, 'What's wrong with it?'

Can you spot any 'dodgy' things about the advertisement? Read it again. Then think. Sandra spotted one or two things. Here they are:

● Bournemouth isn't in Cornwall, it's in Dorset.
● Available 'only to staff employed with this firm' — but why?
● Could it be a terrible squash for eight people?
● The holiday home's rent is really £160 a week, so if there were four people (including children) it would be very expensive.
● No name or address — hiding behind a telephone number — suspicious!

Now you try. Read the newspaper report opposite of a football match between Manchester United and Liverpool. Then make a list of any doubtful items that might lead you to think that the reporter wasn't from Liverpool.

```
A HOLIDAY OF YOUR DREAMS!

A beautiful holiday home is
available for rent, only to
staff employed with this firm.
Situated at Bournemouth in
Cornwall, it's a stone's throw
from the sea.  Plenty of room.
Can take eight people at a
pinch, and very comfortable
for four.  Available from
April to September.  If there
are eight of you, each person
would pay only £20 for a week!
Phone 223344 for details.
```

A great win for United! Liverpool, who strutted onto Old Trafford as if they owned it, were made to look like a rabble by the superb teamwork of a great United team. Roared on by a huge crowd, the Reds tore into their stunned opponents and knocked them for six!

The first goal came just before half-time when 'Tricky' Jimmy Jackson danced past two Liverpool defenders and banged the ball into a gaping net. From then on, nothing could stop the lads!

Liverpool scored a lucky goal in the sixtieth minute when United's keeper, Alex Hands, who'd made several miracle saves, slipped on the greasy turf. That was 1 - 1, with plenty more thrills to come.

United's brilliant attacking play was justly rewarded five minutes from the end of the game, when 'Speedy' Smith outpaced the leaden-footed Liverpool defenders to put the ball firmly in the back of the net. 2 - 1, but it could have been 10 - 1, so superior were United.

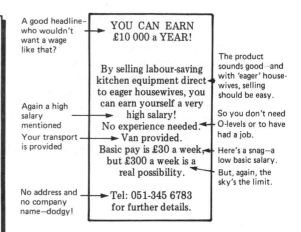

A good headline—who wouldn't want a wage like that?

Again a high salary mentioned

Your transport is provided

No address and no company name—dodgy!

YOU CAN EARN £10 000 a YEAR!

By selling labour-saving kitchen equipment direct to eager housewives, you can earn yourself a very high salary!
No experience needed.
Van provided.
Basic pay is £30 a week, but £300 a week is a real possibility.

Tel: 051-345 6783 for further details.

The product sounds good—and with 'eager' housewives, selling should be easy.

So you don't need O-levels or to have had a job.

Here's a snag—a low basic salary.

But, again, the sky's the limit.

Detective work

Another reading skill is to spot when people try to influence you. This can involve *bias*, where one point of view is presented very strongly. You need to be a detective, to see when you are being influenced by the way something is written or said.

The writer may have a particular point of view. In the football example above, it was obvious that the writer was a Manchester United supporter — the writing supported one side rather than the other. Sports writing is an area where you will often find a particular point of view pressed very strongly. Politics is another area. So too is religion. Can you think of others?

At work you may see evidence of 'loaded' writing. The obvious things to look at are advertisements. Obviously, the writer of an advert is trying to sell something, and the good points will be stressed and the bad ones will be ignored. You wouldn't expect to see 'balanced' writing there. People know and understand how advertising works, and expect to read the 'hard sell' in advertising. 'Hard sell' is unsubtle — it means pushing the customer into buying something by firm, determined selling.

You sometimes see biased writing in job adverts. You should read an advert carefully. Sometimes you have to 'read between the lines' to detect the real message. Look at the example of a job advert shown above.

What are the snags about this job? We've hinted at some of them. Can you think of any others, by 'reading between the lines'? Did you spot the 'loaded' writing?

Skilful advertising persuades people to do all kinds of things, but they usually involve spending money.

The power may be in the words, as in the advert below, but in television and newspapers it is in the pictures too.

Advertisers use words cleverly. They catch your eye. They make you think an idea was yours in the first place. Another technique is

UNBELIEVABLE VALUE

LOOK HERE BEFORE BUYING ELSEWHERE

MANUEL FASHIONS

Bring you
THE BEST IN LEATHER
For
HIM and HER

SHEEPSKINS
JACKETS
TROUSERS
SKIRTS AND
DRESSES

Plus many other fashion accessories

101, HIGH STREET
Tel: 778021

to make customers think 'I can't miss that offer!' or 'I can't manage without it!'

You must read advertisements with great care. Most are honest, giving you accurate information. Many of them exaggerate, as in claims for cars which do sixty miles to the gallon. Others offer a glamorous, exciting, healthy, or safe life — depending on what you buy.

Look at the advert for Manuel Fashions.

What is the attraction to customers?

Now imagine that in your company you have been asked to write an advertisement for the firm or for one of its products. Draft the advert, writing the 'copy' (the words used in the ad), and design the whole thing, using drawings or photographs. If you don't know a company, make one up, such as a car manufacturer or a garage, an electronics firm, or any other one of your choice.

7 Writing processes

You'll have realised by now that being able to write can mean the difference between *getting a job* and *not getting a job*.

In a job, or on a training scheme, writing can also mean the difference between *getting on* and *not getting on*.

These days, many employers look for people who can write down facts and who can pass on information. They want to see this done without fuss and *without mistakes*. They are looking for writing skills — which means the ability to write accurately and correctly.

On the other hand, there are lots of jobs where you won't be asked to do much (or any) writing. Even so, there'll come a time when you have to fill in a job-application form with a covering letter, write a report at work, write a letter to a friend. There's always some writing job to be done, so it's very important to learn the skills.

The key to planning

You should remember from the start of this book that communication follows the pattern of

sender — message — receiver

Writing is no different.

On the other hand, as we saw, breakdowns in communication often happen. This may be because the receiver doesn't understand the message — or, in the case of a written message, can't read it!

To *plan* the message is therefore very important. This means thinking out what you want to say and then planning how you'll say (or write) it. And if it's going to be two-way communication, you have to think about how the receiver will respond.

Here's the key to planning. You have to hold six words in your mind — *what, why, who, when, where, and how*. The message is formed like this:

Here's an example. Read the letter over the page and follow the planning:

What? Jane is after a job with Mr Williams's company.
Why? She went on a visit and was impressed by the company.
Who? She has found out the name of the managing director, Mr Williams.
When? She could visit any time.
Where? At the company offices, of course.
How? She'll phone the company in a day or two.

Let's get this clear: Jane's letter is simple and straightforward, and it's *very clever*. Why? Well, she starts off by thanking Mr Williams for the visit. Then, do you notice that she says the staff were helpful in answering *her* questions. Jane's saying 'I was

27 Hood Street,
Oakley, OY2 1LY

27 May 1985

Dear Mr Williams,

I was one of the group of trainees which visited your company last Friday. Everyone enjoyed the visit, and your staff were very helpful in answering my questions.

I am on a training scheme which finishes in four weeks' time. I am very keen to join your company. Would it be possible for me to see you at a time which suits you, to find out about a possible job? I'll phone in a day or two to see if this could be arranged.

Yours sincerely,

Jane Hopeful.

interested and asked questions — which shows I'm keen.'

Then she gets to the *real message*. The 'thank you' paragraph just got her started! She's after a job, and she gives the essential facts — she finishes her training scheme in four weeks' time. This is her way of telling Mr Williams that she has benefited from training,

work experience, and college. Having asked about a possible job, Jane's not going to be put off by silence — she'll phone in a day or two and pursue Mr Williams.

Now, what about the response? If you were Mr Williams, how would you feel about Jane's letter? How would you reply?

● come in to see me at the offices?

- a letter to say there are no vacancies for jobs?
- a 'thank you' letter to Jane, thanking her for her interest?
- send Jane a list of vacancies and more information about the company?
- or what?

How would *you* respond?

Incidentally, you should notice something else about Jane's letter. It's neatly written; all spellings are correct; and the address, paragraphing, and ending are also correct.

1 What

'What' is the message.

Of course, a letter, a report, or any other kind of writing may have more than one message. There may be a *main* one, a theme, with other messages added on. But a letter to your aunty in Australia with news of all the family doesn't need any *single* message, apart, perhaps, from the fact that everyone is fit and well.

2 Why

Before you start writing, there's the question 'Why do I want to communicate?' to be answered. In a job, the answer is very clear — a reply to a customer, an order to be made out, a letter to the tax inspector, and so on.

'Why?' can often be answered in one of four ways. A written message may

- inform,
- request,
- confirm,
- persuade.

Here are four statements from four different written communications. Which of the four categories would you put them into: request, inform, confirm, persuade?

a) 'I shall be glad to attend the meeting on 23 May.'
b) 'The management has decided that from Monday 6 January new working conditions will apply.'
c) 'Petrol consumption for this car beats all its competitors.'
d) 'Please send ten packs to me at the address above.'

Now try these. let's suppose you are in an office. The boss says to you 'Deal with these three problems by sending a short memo to each of the people concerned.' What is the *reason* — the *why* — behind each one of them? You need to know this before you draft your memos.

a) 'Tell Chris Jones that we won't be able to finish the Nottingham job until December.'
b) 'Look at the job spec for the HYT job. Work out a price and let them know what it is. Send a note to Jack Wales and give him the price and an approximate delivery date.'
c) 'Tell Glenda that we need advertising revenue for the magazine. She has to sell eight pages of advertising at £500 a half-page.'

In each of these memos, you have to pass on *information*. But there's more to it than that. You have to *persuade* people to do things.

This little exercise shows you that written communications can carry several messages, and can have several purposes, too.

3 Who

'Who' is the audience, the receiver. If you know who you are communicating with, you can make the letter personal. That's why in the earlier letter Jane Hopeful did herself a favour by finding out the name of the managing director. If people are written to by name, they are much more likely to reply.

How do you find out? In business, you will often have to write to or phone people you haven't met. Among the questions to be asked, before you start writing, are these:

- What is the name of the person concerned? A phone call to a company could save a lot of time, and get a good response, because you can find out the name of the works manager, the sales director, or whoever you have to write to. Start with the switchboard operator. If you are polite on the phone, you'll get a lot of information and help.
- Is he or she the *right person*? For instance, in writing for a job, the personnel manager could be the person to write to, not the managing director.

```
                                    28 Wilson Hill
                                    Parkley
                                    Manchester    M62 1PW

The Managing Director
Muscle Bodies Ltd              26 March 1985
14 Dodger Street
London   SE28 1PT


Dear Mr Ripoff

In January 1984 I saw an advertisement in the magazine
Your body for a 'Muscleman' kit.  I sent away for it,
paying £50 by cheque.  The kit arrived safely on 2
February.

I followed all the instructions very carefully, although
some of them were not easy.  For eight weeks I did all
the exercises.  I practised every day with the 'Muscleman'
arm-strengthener.  I lay on the floor, stretching and
exercising with the leg-builder.  For thirty minutes
each day I did the chest exercises.  But at the end of the
eight weeks, there was no  improvement at all.  My height
is the same.  My arm, leg, and chest muscles are no larger.
The only thing that did change was my weight, because I
lost ten pounds.

I am returning the 'Muscleman' kit with this letter.  I
should be glad if you would return my £50 to me.  Your
advertisement in last week's copy of Your body says that
if customers aren't satisfied, they can have their money
back.

Yours sincerely

Ivor Smallbody

Ivor Smallbody
```

For an example, let's look at this letter from Ivor Smallbody.

The 'what' and the 'why' of Mr Smallbody's letter should be clear to you. Think about 'who'. Ivor has found out the name of the managing director, so he can write to him personally. Full marks to Ivor!

Now think about the receiver. What kind of person do you imagine Mr Ripoff to be? And what about Ivor? What words would you use to describe him?

Try to answer these questions:

a) What is Mr Ripoff's reaction — his *response* — likely to be?
b) Has Ivor given all the information necessary to his case? Could he have added anything else?

c) Draft a letter from Mr Ripoff in reply to Ivor, giving Muscle Bodies Ltd's answer.

Again, notice that the letter itself is correct: the address of the sender in the top right corner; date; address of the receiver on the left; 'Yours sincerely' at the end of the letter; signed; and with Ivor's name typed out in full below in case his handwriting is unclear.

4   *When*

No communication happens without a time relating to it. For instance, every letter, memo, report, or almost any other kind of writing should have the date on it.

5 Where

Writing also depends on place. You'll learn the difference between a formal business letter for the office, a note left for the next shift in the factory, or an order sent to the grocer.

6 How

'How' means different methods of communication. It can also mean how you say or how you write something. If we stay with writing, there are various forms of writing. You have to learn to choose the appropriate one for the occasion.

Let's look at some examples. What differences can you see in the three pieces below?

What did you notice about them?

- Example A is amusing, light-hearted, with the joke in the last line.
- Example B is formal, pompous, with the humour in the situation, not the writing.
- Example C is all one sentence, and the message isn't even in it (the news that rents were to go up was in the next long complex sentence)!

Obviously, what you learn from this is that *how you write or say something* depends on the circumstances — who you are writing to, the place and time, what you want to say. But there's still no reason (or excuse) for example C above — we should all aim for simple crisp sentences, even if we are city-council officials.

This is all true! We were in our local Kentucky Fried Chicken shop when a boy walked in dressed as a hen. Obviously he was going to a fancy dress party.

The boy said to the girl who was serving, 'Has my sister been in yet?'

'No, but we've just cooked your Mum and Dad,' she said.

A From a letter to a pop magazine

At 11.45 pm you were seen approaching the Town Hall in an unsteady manner. When Constable Brown asked you to explain your movements in the previous hour, you replied, 'Movement, Inspector? I never moved from the Red Lion for three hours. The only movement I made was to lift my beer arm.' At this point, you collapsed into the road-way and caused a public nuisance.

B From a statement read in court

I am writing to inform you that the City Council at their meeting on 26 September 1983, in accordance with the duties imposed on then under Sections 113 and 121 (2a) of the Housing Act, 1957, which required them to review rents and to make such changes, either of the rents generally or of particular rents, as circumstances may require of them, decided that the net rents (exclusive of rates and other charges) of all Council-owned dwellings should continue to be linked to the Gross Rateable Values, and so adopted a general basis of 130% of Gross Rateable Value as the level at which the net rents should be set.

C From a city council office letter to householders, telling them that rents are to be increased.

Now you try

Choose one of the following examples. Write a letter, or a memo, or just a few lines to suit the circumstances.

1   Write to a teenager magazine, telling the editor (and therefore the readers) that you suffer from spots on your face. Does anyone know how to cure them?

2   You have been asked to write a short paragraph for your college tutor about the company, factory, or office where you worked for a short time (it could have been on work experience or a holiday job) or went on a visit. What should you say — how many people worked there? the kind of business they were in? what you thought of the place?

3   You work for a chocolate-making company. A customer has written in to complain that a box of chocolates received as a Christmas present contained stale chocolates. Write a letter of apology to the customer. What else would the company do — send the money back, send another box, or what?

Planning and organising

Planning means preparing — that is, thinking about what you want to say or write, and organising your material in such a way that it's easy to read once you put it down on paper.

Planning and organising involves

● collecting information,
● selecting the relevant bits you need to use,
● organising these in the right order,
● presenting them in a neat letter or memo.

Let's look at the stages.

1   Finding out

You start by collecting the information you'll need. If it's a business letter, you'll need to know all the facts before you start writing. If you don't have all the answers yourself, you have to find out where to go or who to ask to find them.

Let's take an example. Suppose the manager in the company where Gavin works says 'We don't do much business in Manchester. Find out the names and addresses of companies in and around Manchester, so we can write to them, telling them all about the wonders of Marvel's Mouth-watering Foods. Where does Gavin start?

He could go to the local library and ask. They'd tell him to look in the business section. There he might find *Kelly's directory*. This is a list of companies, categorised by area. If they don't have the directory for Manchester, Gavin will have to ask the library to borrow it from another library. Meanwhile, there are other books to search through — a *Register of British manufacturers* and, of course, the *Yellow pages* telephone directory for the Manchester area.

So far, so good. Gavin has found the information he is looking for — in the Manchester area there are about 1400 shops or businesses which sell confectionery or which have canteens which sell chocolate and sweets.

2   Recording the information

Having found the *source* of the information you need (where it is), your next job is to *record* it, or as much of it as you'll need.

The best way of doing this is to take notes. Note-taking is a special art. The skill is in writing the essentials and yet not missing anything of importance.

What do you need? Notes can be made

● in a ruled exercise book,
● in a loose-leaf file (with this method you can add extra pages later),
● on cards (like postcards) — the advantage with this method is that you can shuffle the cards into any order: alphabetical, all the shops in one street, and so on.

Note-taking is very useful when you are preparing a letter or any other business plans. It's also a valuable skill for studying — so that you can take down the essentials from a book, or from a lecture or lesson.

What you do is this:

● read the material — a page of a book, a list of instructions, or whatever — through in full.
● use any headings given and (if it's a letter

or a book) the first and last sentences to give you a sense of what's important.

- Decide on the main points and write them down — you can use your own shorthand, such as 'bk' for 'book', 'Rd' for 'Road', 'mkt' for 'market', and so on.
- Finally, write down any conclusions you have reached.

Now you try. First, decide on a subject in which you are interested. It could be something to do with work (such as computing, job advertisements, or cars). It could be something you are interested in outside work — fashion, music, holidays abroad, etc.

Start by finding out. Go to the local library and find the section where the relevant books are kept — both reference books and books for borrowing.

Choose a book that contains the information you are looking for. Select a topic in it, and make notes on a page from the book. Follow the rules — headings, the main points, the conclusion or opinion at the end. Make up your own shorthand.

3 Organising and arranging

We shall suppose, then, that you have found out where the information is. You've decided which bits you need, and you've made notes on the important items. The next stage is organising or arranging the material to suit your needs.

Let's go back to Gavin. He has discovered the names and addresses of 1400 companies in the Manchester area which have canteens or which are shops that sell chocolate and sweets. 'Well done, Gavin!' says his boss, Mr Grasping, 'Now I want you to draft a letter for me. It's to go with a leaflet which tells people about our marvellous chocolate bars. You write the covering letter, giving them the main facts. Off you go, lad, and let's have the draft in an hour.'

First, Gavin organises. In the letter, he has to say:

- who — who is he writing to — perhaps the managing director;
- why — the reason for the letter;
- what — what it is that Marvel's Mouth-watering Foods have to sell and why the company he's writing to should be interested (this is usually called the 'come-on');
- follow-up — are there any items of information to be added, and who is to sign the letter?

You notice that Gavin is a logical lad — He's listed the ideas in sequence, one after another.

4 Setting out the letter

Gavin drafted the letter for Mr Grasping, and here's how the final version looked.

What do you think of this letter? Judge it along these lines:

- Is it well organised and arranged?
- Would you suggest any changes or improvements?
- Is it *effective* — if you were the managing director of Custards, what would be your reaction to it?

Choose one of the following examples and go through the four stages — finding out, recording the information, selecting and arranging it, and setting it out in a letter or a report.

1 A new scheme of sick pay recently came into operation. Your boss says she's not sure what the new scheme is all about and asks you to write a *one-page report*

Marvel's Mouth-watering Foods Ltd

Sweet Lane
Nottingham, NG2 1LG
Telephone: Nottingham 2345

Who? —
start with
the
Managing
Director

The Managing Director
Custards Ltd.
Pie Street   19th September 1984
Manchester M32 1SW

Dear Sir

Why? —
introducing
Marvel's

I'm sure that you've heard of Marvel's chocolates and sweets.
They are very popular, especially with young people. For
instance, last year we sold over 300 000 'Choc-o-Lumps',
the munchy chocolate bar which has been advertised on television.

What? —
explains the
leaflet

I am enclosing a leaflet which tells you all about our products.
As you can see, they include all kinds of sweets, and many
different chocolate blends. Another very popular line is
'Lolly Choc-ice', and last year we topped a million sales of
these.

You can also benefit from these marvellous sales.
Why not put our sweets and chocolates on sale in your shop
or your canteen? I can assure you that your profits will
show a big improvement.

What's in
it for you

On the leaflet you will find details of the wholesale
prices. In addition, there are the recommended retail prices
when the goods go on sale. As you will see,
your profit could be forty per cent.

Follow-up

Our representative will call on you in a week or two
to take your orders: we are sure you won't want to miss this
opportunity.

Yours faithfully

A. Grasping

Signing off

Albert Grasping
Sales Manager

about it. There's a special leaflet (NI 244) which explains the new scheme. You can get this from any DHSS office. Write the report, following the four rules that you've learned in this section of the book.

2 You decide to go to Europe on your annual holiday this year. Choose how you'll go — by car, by train, or on a package holiday by air.

Then, find out about the different kinds of holiday from the brochures in travel agents. Write a *summary* of what you find out. Follow the four rules and deal with where, when, how, costs, advantages and disadvantages, and any other information which you think is needed.

3 You are thinking about what kind of job you'd like to do. Choose one. Then find out about it from careers leaflets and from books. Next, assemble the facts, choosing and selecting those which you think are important. On one side of a piece of paper, set out these facts in a *report*. It should deal with what's involved in doing the job, entry qualifications, training, pay, promotion, and anything else you think is important.

8 Writing techniques

The actual amount of writing you'll do depends on the kind of job you have. Obviously, if you are in an office, there'll be a lot of paperwork. If you work outdoors or in a workshop or factory, there won't be so much writing as part of the job.

On the other hand, everyone has to do *some* kind of writing — there will be letters, notes, shopping lists, team-sheets, and so on.

To start with, then, let's look at the kinds of writing you may have to do, both in the course of a job and after work — that is, at home or as part of your leisure time.

- *Getting a job* Applying for a job involves some writing. You may have to fill in an application form, and possibly write a letter to the employer, too.
- *Making notes* In the previous chapter, you learned how to make notes for a report. There are other kinds of note, too — such as a note for the milkman, a note in the office diary, a note for someone following you on a machine.
- *Reports* These come *after* you've got a job. Reports are of all kinds, dealing with the firm's business. But there are other reports — you may be involved in a road accident, or be a witness to one. You may have to write 'a report' for an insurance company if you lose something valuable.
- *Minutes* Minutes are the official records of a meeting. Secretaries have to be good at writing minutes. In a way, writing minutes is similar to note-writing, where you have to summarise the main points.
- *Letters* First, there are the business letters you might have to write. If you are in an office, you'll be shown the right way and the wrong way to do this. But there are letters, too, about your own

business — letters to the council, to a bank, to your insurance company, and so on.
- *Personal writing* You may keep a diary — that is one kind of 'personal' writing. Other kinds could be letters to your friends, or stories, or poems.

Applying for a job

Many job adverts ask you to telephone to arrange an interview. However, some ask you to write a letter, applying for the job. Along with the letter, you may have to complete a job-application form. Let's look at both of them.

Here's a typical advertisement in a newspaper.

Big Box Co Ltd
Machine Operator
We are looking for school leavers to train as machine operators. Apply in writing to Mrs Bird, Personnel Manager, Big Box Co., 13 Sea Road, Liverpool. L21 2AS

Every time you write a letter, you show something of yourself. A letter can show your attitudes as well as your ability (especially at English). So, when you write applying for a job, you must make a very good impression. The way the letter is set out is important. So, too, are spelling and grammar.

What an employer looks for

- Neat handwriting
- Correct spelling
- Helpful information about you
- Correct addresses (yours and the firm's)
- Personal details such as
  schools
  qualifications
  training (YTS etc.)
  job or work experience

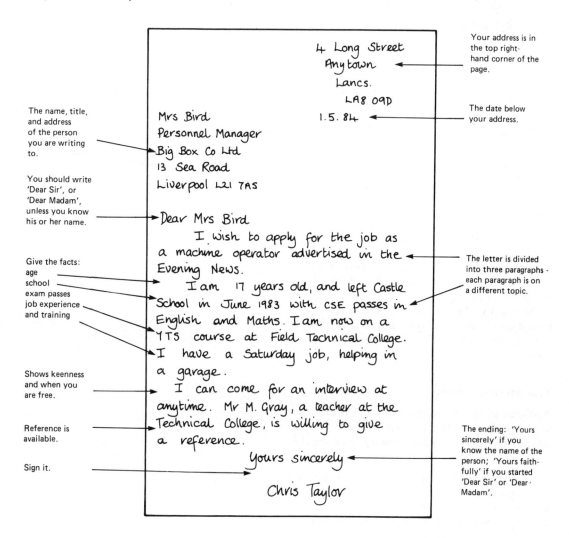

Your address is in the top right-hand corner of the page.

The name, title, and address of the person you are writing to.

You should write 'Dear Sir', or 'Dear Madam', unless you know his or her name.

The date below your address.

Give the facts:
age
school
exam passes
job experience
and training

The letter is divided into three paragraphs - each paragraph is on a different topic.

Shows keenness and when you are free.

Reference is available.

Sign it.

The ending: 'Yours sincerely' if you know the name of the person; 'Yours faithfully' if you started 'Dear Sir' or 'Dear Madam'.

---

4 Long Street
Anytown
Lancs.
LA8 09D
1.5.84

Mrs Bird
Personnel Manager
Big Box Co Ltd
13 Sea Road
Liverpool L21 7AS

Dear Mrs Bird
        I wish to apply for the job as a machine operator advertised in the Evening News.
        I am 17 years old, and left Castle School in June 1983 with CSE passes in English and Maths. I am now on a YTS course at Field Technical College. I have a Saturday job, helping in a garage.
        I can come for an interview at anytime. Mr M. Gray, a teacher at the Technical College, is willing to give a reference.
                Yours sincerely

                Chris Taylor

Choose one of the advertisements below and write a letter applying for the job, following the advice already given. Make sure that you set out the letter properly.

Sales Person Wanted

Keen sales person required to sell household and garden equipment. Could be full-time or part-time work. No experience needed, as full training will be given.

Write to the Manager,
Temple's Ltd,
345 Long Road,
Newcastle-on-Tyne 4

Do You Enjoy Outdoor Work?

If you do, write to Pearsons with full details of any experience or training you've had, your education, and why you'd like to work in the open:

Mr Eric Bland,
Personnel Manager,
Pearsons Ltd.,
High Street,
Hull HL21 1DR

Handy's

Need school leavers to work in one of several departments:

- sales
- distribution
- messengers
- office

Write with full details about yourself to
Mrs J Needy,
Handy's Ltd,
Willson Road,
Glasgow GS7 5HS

Application forms

Instead of writing a general letter applying for a job, you may have to fill in an application form sent you by the firm. Like the letter, this requires a lot of skill to complete properly.

On a form, many personal details have to be put down. Here is an example of a form that's been correctly filled in. Study it carefully.

Your personal record

Application forms are important. Filling them in can be the key to a job. As well as following the advice given above, you should also:

- read the form through before you start to complete it;
- write or print neatly;
- complete it lightly in pencil first, then go over it in black ink or ballpoint;
- make sure you put down all your qualifications, work experience, training, and any special skills you have.

As you can see, it's important to have all the facts about yourself organised in a clear pattern. Sometimes, a company will just say

Frames Ltd

APPLICATION FORM

Surname: _JOHNSON_

First or Christian names: _MARY_

Home Address: _14, LIME LANE, ARKLEY SOUTHAMPTON, SN2 1LZ_

In full, with the postcode

Telephone number: _ARKLEY 261_   Nationality: _BRITISH_

If you have one

Date and place of birth: _16th MAY 1967, LONDON_

Name and address of parent or guardian: _MR O. JOHNSON (FATHER)_

14. LIME LANE, ARKLEY, SOUTHAMPTON, SN2 1LZ

Secondary schools attended and dates: _HILLTOP SCHOOL, SOUTHAMPTON_
_1978 - 1983_

Sometimes they ask about primary schools too

Exams with grades: GCE: _ENGLISH (GRADE C)_

CSE: _ENGLISH (GRADE 1) GEOGRAPHY (2) WOODWORK (3) MATHS (4)_

Other: _RSA : TYPING - PASS_

Give subjects and grades or, if you are waiting for results, when they are expected

Date when you take exams (or expect results): _✓_

Previous employment (including part-time or holiday jobs): _I HAVE HAD A SATURDAY_
JOB IN A SHOP AND HAVE BEEN ON WORK EXPERIENCE AT DAVIS STORES
SOUTHAMPTON, FOR 12 WEEKS

All work experience is important

Are you willing to take further training: _YES_

Reason for applying: _I'VE ALWAYS WANTED TO WORK IN AN OFFICE OR STORE._

A chance to show you are keen

References — name and address of a suitable person: _MR .F. THOMAS,_

11 WILLIAM STREET, ARKLEY (TEACHER AT MY SCHOOL)

Ask first, before you put someone's name on a form

Have you suffered from any serious illness (give illness and year): _____

DERMATITIS , 1974

Any special skills or training: _I AM NOW ON A YTS CLERICAL SKILLS COURSE_
WHICH ENDS IN JUNE

They are looking for a disability, skin condition etc.

Interests: _YOUTH CLUB, TENNIS, MUSIC_

YTS or any other kind of training is a big advantage

Signature: _Mary Johnson_   Date: _14th APRIL 1985._

CURRICULUM VITAE

PERSONAL DETAILS
Name   Karen Poole
Address   20 Rose Street, Woodley, Warwickshire WY2 8XA
Telephone   Woodley (0234) 29282
Date of birth   10th June 1967   Age now: 17yrs 2mths

EDUCATION AND
QUALIFICATIONS
Secondary Schools   Sept 1977 - April 1979: Langley Comprehensive, Manchester
                     May 1979 - July 1983: Woodley School, Long Road, Woodley
Examinations   CSE: English (grade 1), Commerce (grade 2)
                          Biology (grade 3), History (grade 4).
School interests   Member of school choir. Sport: member of
                     school tennis team. Swimming: bronze medal for
                     life saving.

WORK EXPERIENCE   Jan to July 1983: paper round for NSS Newspapers,
AND TRAINING   High Street, Woodley.
                     Sept 1983 to date: Youth Training Scheme, including
                     12 weeks in the offices of CARE Computers Ltd.
                     The scheme also included 12 weeks at Pilton
                     College of further Education for off-the-job training.

INTERESTS   I am a member of the local youth club and go
                     swimming with club members. I enjoy discos and
                     dancing. I can type 40 words per minute and
                     learned office skills during the YTS course.

HEALTH   Very good. Broken arm in 1977 and glandular fever
                     in 1983.

AMBITIONS   Eventually I would like to have a job where I can
                     help people, such as in the Social Services or
                     hospitals

REFERENCE   Mr Alan Brand, Training Officer, CARE Computers
                     Ltd., Industrial Estate, Broadoak, Warwicks,
                     BK1 0AP

68

'Send your c.v.' 'C.V.' is short for 'curriculum vitae' — a Latin phrase which means 'the story of your life'. It's used to summarise the same information which goes on an application form. You can see opposite how Karen Poole set out her c.v. It's a very good model for you to follow.

Write your own c.v.

On a large sheet of paper, summarise the information about yourself. This is an exercise in planning and organisation, and it's particularly useful because it's about you and it will help you to get a job.

You should summarise the information under these headings:

1 Pesonal — your name, date of birth, address, telephone number.
2 Schools and colleges attended, with dates, and all your exam passes and qualifications, including grades.
3 Any jobs (including part-time and holiday ones) and training.
4 Your interests — hobbies, sporting activities and clubs.
5 The names of two people in positions of responsibility — your headteacher or course tutor — said they will be willing to give you a reference, if they are asked for one.
6 Your health record.
7 Your ambitions — what you hope for in the future; what courses you'd like to take; what job you'd like to do.

Writing at work

The next group of assignments and examples is taken from the world of work.

When you start work, in a new place, and with strangers, you feel nervous and tense. There seems a lot to learn — new routines, new skills, new words, and new ways of doing things. And — unlike at school, where teaching is built around *you*, the pupil — at work the important thing is the *job*, production, the service, or whatever the company is doing.

First, language. Here is a list of words you may have to use in the first days at work. What do they mean? Match the words to the phrases below them, and see how many you can get right.

1 Supervisor
2 Shop-steward
3 Contract
4 Overtime
5 Schedule
6 Word-processor
7 Shift
8 Bonus
9 Deadline
10 Union card
11 Distribution
12 Deductions
13 Clocking-on
14 Block release
15 Brochure

A A written agreement between two or more people, such as an employer and an employee
B The latest time by which a job has to be completed
C The membership card of someone in a trade union
D A continuous period of time spent training at a college, such as six weeks
E A leaflet which describes the company's products or services
F A system for registering the time when people start work
G Extra money earned by high output, or given at holiday times or Christmas
H A set period of the day for work, such as 8 a.m. to 2 p.m.
I The person in charge of a section or a group of workers
J A plan of work, often with timings by which special jobs have to be done
K Money taken from your wages for tax, insurance, etc.
L A small computer for storing information used in the office
M A system for sending materials or goods from the factory or shop to customers
N A representative of a union, elected by other members in a firm or section
O Hours worked over or beyond the agreed minimum hours of work

Short notes and messages

In your work you may be asked to write short notes and messages, and to make summaries from technical reports. Here are some examples.

1 'Kevin's had to go out for the day. Let him know tomorrow's meeting is off, but I'll need his sales figures at nine o'clock.'

2 'Linda, send a memo to the buyer, telling her to order three steel filing cabinets. I phoned yesterday, so she knows the order is on its way.'

3 'Michael has had to go home because his wife is ill. Write a note for the next shift, telling them what has to be done.'

Notes are an informal way of communicating. On the other hand, they can be very important, for they can keep the flow of work moving smoothly. It is just as important as in a letter to write down the correct information and — if the note is handwritten — to make sure it can be easily read!

Memos are similar to notes. They tend to be internal messages within a company. They are a written record, sometimes of a telephone conversation. Like the note, you don't have to start 'Dear Sir' nor end 'Yours sincerely'. They should be kept short, and usually deal with only one item of information. Three things are essential: the name of the sender, the name of the person to whom the memo is sent, and the date it is sent.

Now, as an example, here's the note that Linda sent.

🎩 Memorandum

To	L. Newhouse, Chief Buyer
From	W. Turner, Training Manager
Date	19.9.83

Subject: Filing Cabinets

Please order for this department three new filing cabinets. They should have three sections and be lock-able. They are urgently needed. Deliver to Room 67. This order confirms the phone call made on 18.9.83.

What do you think of this note? What would you say about the style of the message?

Try these

Write two notes. They should be for examples 1 and 3 above. You can make up the other details.

Reports

One day, your boss might turn to you and say 'Will you write a report on it?' Where do you start?

It sounds a terrible job, but it needn't be. Report-writing is a skill, like any other communication skill, and you need practice at it. But it's not really any different to other 'formal' kinds of writing — essays, memos, articles. You probably find that the thought of writing essays fill you with dread and horror anyway, so we'd better look at report-writing. You never know — one of these days you might *volunteer* to write a report!

A report is a written communication containing information or advice. It need not be long, and it shouldn't be complicated. It is usually written by someone who has done a survey or carried out an inquiry — someone who knows the *facts*. It is usually sent from the writer to the receiver for *action*.

Let's look at an example. From what we've said above, you should realise that a report should

- contain facts and information,
- expect some action as the result of it,
- be written in a simple concise style which is easy to read,
- be accurate.

How does the report below measure up?

Here's the situation. Alison Rosewell is the secretary to the managing director of Jasper's Manufacturing Co. Ltd. Alison hears complaints in the canteen that women working in the factory are being paid less than the men, and that some women are being asked to work extra hours. She tells her boss, Mr Shields, the managing director. He says 'I'm too busy to deal with that, Alison. Find out what's happening and write a short report for me.'

Here's what Alison wrote.

What do you think? Did Alison's report follow the rules of report-writing? The answer is yes, it did. Alison was concise, she

R E P O R T

For the attention of Mr John   From: Alison Rosewell
Shields, Managing Director   Date: 15 June 1985

1 Terms of Reference

Following complaints by women working at Jasper's Manufacturing
Co. Ltd, to find out if women are being unfairly treated, and to
make a report to the managing director.

2 Procedure

To find out the facts, I did the following:
a) talked to men and women working in the factory and in other
    parts of the company, such as the canteen, offices, and on
    maintenance work;
b) talked to the shop-steward and trade-union officials;
c) read leaflets and found out about equal treatment for men and
    women under the law.

3 Findings

A The law   a) Since 1975, when the Sex Discrimination
                  Act became law, it has been illegal to
                  discriminate against or treat unfairly
                  women who are in employment.
              b) Since the Equal Pay Act of 1970, it has been
                  against the law to pay a woman less than a
                  man for doing the same job, or one that is
                  broadly similar.
              c) It is against the law (the Employment Acts)
                  to ask either men or women to work more hours
                  than in their contract of employment, unless
                  agreed rates for overtime are paid.

B The factory a) The rates of pay for production and other jobs
                  are the same for both men and women, when
                  they are doing the same work.
              b) There are unskilled jobs, which are on a
                  different grade, where the pay is less. As
                  it happens, all of these jobs are held by
                  women.
              c) If men or women work extra hours, they are
                  paid more money at the agreed rates.

4 Recommendations

1 A memo should be sent to everyone working at Jasper's,
   explaining that the company believes it treats men and women
   equally and fairly under the terms of the law.
2 However, if anyone has a complaint, they should raise it first
   with the shop steward or the company welfare officer.
3 The company should look at the grades and the pay of unskilled
   workers, with a view to increasing the wages of the people (all
   of them being women) who are in these grades.

Signed ...Alison Rosewell...

kept to the point, she found out the facts, and she called for action by the managing director.

Jasper's comes out of her inquiry quite well. There's no deliberate discrimination in the company. On the other hand, it looks as if some jobs (all held by women) could do with regrading and better pay. This is probably where the problem arose in the first place. And, lastly, Alison did the right thing by asking the opinion of the trade-union people.

You should notice something else about Alison's report. Look at how it's set out. Not only did Alison find out about equal pay, she also discovered some of the rules of report-writing:

Terms of reference

Before you start to write, you need to know exactly what it is you are covering, and why. The terms of reference define the scope of the inquiry and the report.

The 'terms' should state the *authority* for the report — that is, who has asked for it, in this case the managing director.

Procedure

This describes how you set about finding out the facts. It might have been by reading books and leaflets, interviewing or talking to people, visiting, or observing.

Findings

This should be the main body of the report. It should contain the detailed information which has been collected and classified. You'll notice that Alison has divided her findings into two groups — the law and the factory.

Conclusions and recommendations

At the end comes a section which summarises the main findings. Alison missed this out because her report was short and to the point anyway. In the recommendations, the writer explains how the problem may be solved. This is the 'action' part of the report.

Report-writing can be a lot more complicated than this. If you are promoted in a company, you may be asked to write longer and more complex reports. At this stage in your career or work, however, Alison's example is fully adequate.

Now you try. Write a short report, setting it out as Alison did, on one of these topics:

1   There has been a lot of vandalism and noise on your estate or in your street. Write a report to the chairman of the council about it, giving some suggestions for action.
2   Write a report of no more than 300 words on any aspect of your work or your studies. The report is to your tutor, and might make suggestions for changes or improvements.
3   Let's imagine that you are working in a hotel. There have been some complaints by customers that the bedrooms haven't been properly or promptly cleaned and tidied. The manager asks you to investigate and write a report. Write it!

Letters

In the previous chapter and in this one you have already studied several letters. You will have noticed that letter-writing has its own rules.

To test your knowledge so far, how many things are wrong with the letter opposite?

● The address doesn't include the postcode.
● The date is missing.
● The manager's name is probably 'Mrs Harris', so there's a spelling error.
● 'A job' is vague — what job, and what 'paper'? Mrs Harris might have ten jobs to offer in different advertisements.
● What course? What college?
● Another spelling mistake — it should be 'Yours sincerely'.

A letter like Billy's has no chance of success. Mrs Harris would say 'He's no good. He can't spell. He doesn't think. He's careless.' and so on.

Let's look at the rules.

Business letters (and a letter applying for a job is a business letter) should be:

● clear,
● brief,

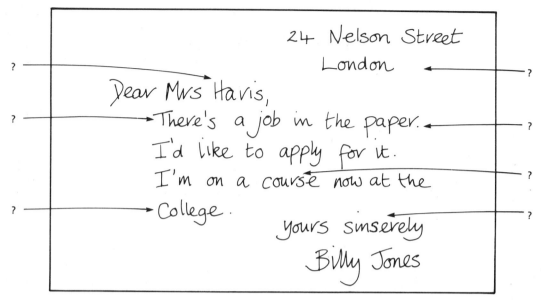

24 Nelson Street
London

Dear Mrs Havis,

There's a job in the paper.
I'd like to apply for it.
I'm on a course now at the
College.

yours sinserely
Billy Jones

? ? ? ? ? ? ?

- informative (the facts),
- properly set out
- correctly spelt and grammatical.

The letter on the next page obeys the rules:

Read the letter through. Then look for these parts which show that it is correctly written:

- *The 'salutation' or opening* If the writer was writing to someone he or she knew personally, this could be 'Dear Mr Brown'. You would only use 'Dear Bill' if you knew the reader of the letter very well indeed.
- *The sender's address* Placed in the top right-hand corner, unless there is a printed address heading.
- *The date* All letters should have the date, usually put under the sender's address.
- *Reference* Letters often have to be filed or coded, and the reference gives this information, often in the form of the writer's initials, then the secretary's initials, and an order number if there is one.
- *The receiver's address* Usually placed above 'Dear Sir or Madam' on the left-hand side.
- *Telephone number*
- *Signature* 'Yours faithfully' is usually for formal letters. 'Yours sincerely' is used for letters where the addressee's name is

known and used, such as 'Dear Mr Brown'. Notice that Ron Worried signs the letter. His name has also been typed (in case his signature can't be read), and his job title, 'Manager', has been added.
- *Enclosure* There is an order form which is enclosed with the letter and 'Enclosure' is added by the secretary to remind him or her (and the reader) to look for and read it.
- *The letter* There is only one paragraph because there is only one main topic. If another main point needed to be raised, there would be a second paragraph.
- *Style* The letter is brisk and to the point.

But, lastly, what does the letter tell you about the business that is being done? Mr Worried is putting in an order for furniture. But he is uneasy. How can you tell? What does he want Witton Ltd to do, apart from sending all the furniture?

Write your own business letter

Choose one of the examples below and write a letter, set out like those already given in this book.

1 Imagine that you are the secretary of a local sports club. It could be football, cricket, tennis, or another sport. Write a letter to a supplier, ordering goods for the club. Explain how the supplier will be paid, and ask for discounts. Add an inquiry about delivery dates.

Knockdown Furniture Stores

Woodworm House
Green Lane
Northley
Bristol BS21 2AS
Northley 7856

```
Sales Manager
Wilton Ltd
PO Box 21
Bigley
Surrey    BY2 9DF


Our reference:  FGK/SD/Order 321        14 January 1984


Dear Sir

        I enclose an official order for the purchase and
delivery, as soon as possible, of 20 wardrobes, 35 single
beds, 42 chairs and 15 tables.  As agreed with Mr Flash
by telephone, these items of furniture are at a discount price
of 25 per cent.  I should be glad if you would confirm in
writing that the selling prices are as shown in your catalogue,
minus the discount.

Yours faithfully

Ron. Worried

Ron Worried
Manager

Enclosure
```

2 Suppose you have your own business. Design your own letter-head with the name of your business, the address, and the telephone number. Then write a letter to one of your customers, offering your services. Explain what it is you have to sell, and say how useful your service or goods could be.

3 Write a letter to the local bus company, explaining that you left something on a bus. Give all the details — the day and time, the bus route, the object you left behind, what it looks like, and so on. Tell them how you can be contacted.

Other writing

Memos, reports, notes, questionnaires, letters — these are all methods of written communication. There are also other ways of passing on messages. There isn't space in this book to deal with them all, and in any case most of them are *office* tasks, connected with business companies. You'd learn the skills of writing minutes, telex messages, reply cards, advertisements, and questionnaires as part of training for office jobs. In this book we are concerned mainly with writing as part of your entry into work.

Let's therefore look at two more writing tasks linked to your first job and the training you could be given as part of the job.

An accident

In 1974 an Act of Parliament was passed which set out the duties of employers and employees regarding health and safety. When you start work, the safety precautions that have to be taken will be explained to you.

All the same, accidents do happen at work. Tim and Irene were two trainees working in a factory. One day, they arrived at work to find Jack Briggs, a workman, lying unconscious. They raised the alarm, and Jack was taken away to hospital. Later, the safety officer asked them to write a short report, explaining what had happened. Tim and Irene started by writing down, in any order, the things that happened. Here's their list.

1   Jack was lying flat on his back, unconscious.
2   We arrived for work together.
3   Irene ran straight to the office and phoned for an ambulance.
4   It must have been nine o'clock when we went into the workshop.
5   Tim knew where the mains switch was and switched off the power.
6   We tried first-aid, as we had been shown, until the ambulance arrived.
7   I went to the locker room first, to put on my overalls — that took about five minutes.
8   Lying beside Jack was a screwdriver. It seemed as if he'd been trying to repair one of the electric motors.
9   Tim loosened Jack's collar so he could breathe more easily.
10 As we went into the workshop, I said to Tim that there was a smell of burning.

What you have to do is to write a report putting their description of what happened into the right order of events.

The right gear

When you start work, it is important to know what kind of clothes to wear. Usually the firm will tell you. But some companies don't bother, and you could turn up for work in quite the wrong gear.

Make a list of six jobs (such as painter or cook) where special clothing is needed. In each case, say what the special clothing is.

Then make a list of another five jobs where special headgear is needed. Say what kind of hat or helmet is needed, and why.

Next, here's what a company told its employees about what to wear at work. The notice below was pinned up on the board.

```
        JIMMY'S JAM BUTTY FACTORY

          Rules about clothing

Before entering the factory, all employees
must observe the health and safety rules, which
include instructions about the clothing to be
worn.

1   All employees must wear a white overall and
    white hat.

2   Outdoor shoes or boots must be removed:
    employees are to wear the special slippers
    provided.

3   Personal clothing (coats, hats, shoes etc.)
    should be placed in the locker.

4   Visitors and employees must wash and dry
    their hands thoroughly in the cloakroom
    before entering the factory.

5   Failure to observe these rules will lead to
    dismissal.
```

What do you think of this notice? Does it communicate the message clearly? Can you see any problems looming up for the management and the employees?

It may not be a perfect notice, but it certainly tells people what is expected of them.

Now it's your turn. The problem is this. You are the manager of a store. The employees have been turning up for work in all kinds of gear: jeans, suits, open-necked shirts, fashion boots, and so on. You don't want to make everyone wear the same thing — a uniform of some kind. On the other hand, you want all the sales staff to be smart, and dressed in a similar way.

You've decided on the new rules. You must now explain what you want them to wear. Draft your communication to the staff. What will you say, and how will you say it? You can choose any one of these methods of written communication: a notice, a memo, a letter to each member of staff, or any method you can think of.

9 Visual communication

At work, as outside it, you will be bombarded with examples of *visual communication*. 'Visual' means conveying information and impact through the eyes, sometimes without words, sometimes with words.

Advertising is an example of visual communication. Advertisers realise the value of using drawings, cartoons, photographs, and other eye-catching illustrations to attract people's attention. On television and at the cinema we see brilliant examples of visual communication, too.

The object of commercial advertising is often to sell something. But visual communication may also be used to illustrate information (through a chart or a graph) or to show dramatic events or emotions (as in films). Whatever the method used though, there is the same overall objective as in other forms of communication — the *sender* despatches a *message*, and hopes to awaken a *response* in the *receiver*.

1   The cartoon above was in a national newspaper. A famous company had reported a big loss of business and therefore of profits.

    a)   What do you think is the message?
    b)   What effect would it have on two receivers: (i) the newspaper readers who might be thinking of investing in this company, (ii) the managing director of the company?

2   The drawing opposite illustrates a safety campaign, designed to get workers on building sites used to wearing helmets.

    a)   What is the message?
    b)   Is it effective?

3   Pick one of the topics from the list below. Draw a cartoon without words, or with

only one or two words, to illustrate the topic. Remember that there has to be a message in the drawing.

a) Using safety belts in cars.
b) Contributing to a charity (you choose which one).
c) 'Your best buy this week is . . . .'

Advertising

Advertisers fully recognise the importance of visual communication. You see evidence of it in newspapers, magazines, television, posters, and in many other ways.

What is an advertisement? Can you define it? Here is one description:

● An advertisement is a message, paid for by people who want to send it, and intended to inform or influence people in general.

You'll notice that the key words in this definition are ones you have already met — message, sender, inform, influence, receiver. There is another key phrase. — 'paid for'. Most advertising has to be paid for, but not all of it. Think of ways that youth clubs, schools, colleges, and charities advertise — they don't always have to pay for it because they can often obtain volunteers to help them.

Let's look at some adverts to see how they work.

Below is a famous advertisement for baked beans? What makes it effective? The answer is

a) the company name — Heinz is a well known food company, and everyone knows the linked phrase 'Heinz Beans';
b) the slogan — notice the clever alteration of 'Beans' to 'Beanz' and 'Means' to 'Meanz';
c) the simple but effective illustration.

Slogans are often used in advertising because they are catchy, short, and make you smile. Think of others. What's the ending to 'A Mars a day . . .'?

Now look at the advert for the Youth Training Scheme. What do you think of it? Is it effective? If so, how?

Now you try

Here are some imaginary brand names. What products do you think they could go with? Make up slogans to advertise them, and then draw an advert for each one:

- Smart
- Whizzo
- Dreamy
- Flying High

The Youth Training Scheme will take a great weight off a mother's shoulders.

And off her mind. Because any parent with a 16 year old son or daughter who's leaving school soon must be worried about their children's prospects. Particularly in the current economic climate.

The Youth Training Scheme is a chance for teenagers to learn basic work skills before they launch themselves into the fiercely competitive world of job hunting. Skills which will improve their prospects of landing a worthwhile job later on.

Every 16 year old school-leaver can go on the scheme. So can some 17 year olds. They will all be given a year of planned work experience and training.

And when they've completed the scheme, they'll receive a signed certificate which employers will value as proof of their achievements. It's worth more than money.

So what about the alternatives? Hanging around in amusement arcades? Or around your neck? Or worse? If it's a problem that's weighing heavily on your mind your local Careers Office or Job-centre can give advice which will help to lessen the burden.

Youth Training Scheme

If they don't get on the Youth Training Scheme, how are they going to get on?

People who advertise . . . and why they do it

Before you can decide how effective an advertisement is, you must think about *who* is doing the advertising, and *why* they do it.

Can you think of any other people who advertise (who) and the product, service, or other reason for doing so (why)? Add them to the list. On the right, some of the 'how' spaces are empty. Complete the third column of entries on a separate sheet of paper.

Who	Why	How
Industries and companies	To sell their goods and services. To recruit staff to work for them. To give information about a product.	Posters, TV, radio (local and national commercial)
Organisers of events	To tell people about sports events, concerts, what's on at the cinema or theatre.	
Colleges	To give information about courses.	Prospectuses
Political parties and pressure groups	To win people's votes or their support.	
Charities	To get money or help.	Leaflets Flag days
The government	To provide information about new laws and rights. To explain about local or government services. To make people think about health and safety.	Television, newspapers
The press and television	To attract readers or viewers. To sell advertising space or time.	
The public	To sell or buy goods. To let or rent houses or flats.	Newspapers

Effective advertising

You should have noticed that effective advertising (that is, getting the message across) often involves *both* words and pictures. These have to be carefully chosen to attract and to influence the people who read or look at the adverts. Advertisers call the words they use in an advertisement the 'copy'. This can be very short — pehaps only a word or two — or a slogan, or it may be a little story.

The illustrations (*pics* or pictures) should add to the advert. Between them, the *copy* and the *pics* contain the essence of the message.

Below is an advert from a local newspaper. Do you think it is effective? If so, how? If not, how would you sell Sandra's hairdressing service? Write new copy and draw a pic to illustrate it.

Need a haircut, shampoo, set or styling?

No time to get your hair done, then you ought to ring me immediately.
Have your hair done in your own home.
Ring Sandra
at 267511

The best of the new

Look at a magazine or a newspaper. Listen to commercial radio or television. How often do they use the words 'best', 'new', 'bargain'? You will find that these words are used time after time.

Make a list of other key words used by advertisers. Why are they used? Are some words more effective in advertising than others? What words would advertisers *not* use?

Another technique used in advertising is 'before and after'. You see this in adverts for soap, shampoos, clothes, and other personal goods. Often the comparison is exaggerated, as in the cartoon above.

A third way in which copy is skilfully written and used with pictures is to disguise the real message. For example, if people are fat, or ugly, or stupid, or all three, advertisers don't tell the truth. They use words such as 'mature' for 'old', and 'fuller figure' for 'fat'.

Match the words or phrases on the left with those on the right.

- Receding hairline
- Face blemish
- Unwanted hair
- Personal problem
- Slender

- Skinny
- Bald
- Body smell
- Wart
- Moustache

Design, draw, and write an advertisement for one of these products:

- new sports equipment,
- a new perfume,
- a new line in men's or women's clothes.

A picture is worth a thousand words . . .

If you look through a colour magazine, some of the advertisements immediately catch your attention. What are the factors which attract you, hold your attention, and persuade you to read the copy?

Select three adverts in a magazine:

- Write down the attraction of each advert.
- Which one is the most effective? Why?

Your answers are likely to include some mention of the picture used in the advert. In effective advertising it is the *graphics* (photographs, drawings, diagrams) which make the impact. They attract attention, often because of their startling use of colour. A glossy magazine such as a weekly or monthly may carry 200 advertisements. The ones likely to catch attention are those with colour and dramatic impact. You can see this in adverts for cars, food, clothes, houses, electrical goods, and many more products. You should also notice that really effective adverts use few words. As we noted at the beginning of this chapter, it is the *visual* impact which is important.

The target audience

In all forms of communication, it is essential to think of the receiver. In the case of visual communication on radio and television and through newspapers and magazines, the receiver is the *audience or readership*.

Most advertisements are planned to appeal to a certain kind of person. This is the *target audience*. The words, phrases, and pictures are carefully chosen to appeal to this audience.

The company or organisation you work for or are planning to join should have a clear idea of its target audience. It may be young people, the elderly, or children. It could be a particular group — car-owners, house-buyers, or computer enthusiasts.

Look through several advertisements and decide on the target group for each one. When you have done that, design an advert (with illustrations and copy) for footwear for each of these groups of people:

● young children,
● teenage girls,
● mountain-climbers.

Collect examples of adverts, brochures, or other kinds of printed material from a company or organisation you know or have worked for. Explain how they have been designed for a particular audience.

The image

Every company wants to have a 'good image'. This means that people think well of it and say 'That's a good company — you can trust them.'

Another kind of image is through *impact*. For instance, if a company wants the general public to buy a particular product, it tries to stamp its image on people's minds.

One way of doing this is through the company's 'logo'. This is a symbol. Among examples are British Rail's sign, the Esso

tiger, and the Lloyd's Bank horse.

Another way is by dramatic visual illustration. You see this in advertising where glamour or wealth are stressed in order to sell a product. You see this in adverts for cars and perfume, but also in many other kinds of advertising.

Those of you with driving ambition are urged to apply now!

We at Lotus are delighted to announce a modest increase in production of both Excel and Esprit, without any reduction in Lotus' race proven excellence.

Of course we are not rivalling our so-called rivals' levels of mass production (Porsche, Mercedes and BMW between them make in excess of 18,000 cars a week).

If we did, a Lotus wouldn't have the exclusivity of a Lotus.

But currently a limited number of

crisp and gleaming new Excels and Esprits is available for discerning buyers who want the best.

Apply to join us now
Call 0272 277007 and we'll put you in touch with the supply line. With no obligation.

But please act immediately – Lotus cars don't hang around – and neither should their owners.

LOTUS CARS LIMITED NORWICH NORFOLK ENGLAND NR14 8EZ

Think of a product or service. The product could be something advertised on television. The service could be a shop, a garage, a hairdresser. Design, draw, and write the copy for a one-page description of it. You could also design a logo. To create the image, you might stress one (or more) of these:

- glamour,
- money,
- ambition,
- humour,
- good health,
- fantasy.

Non-verbal communication

In this chapter we have looked at how illustrators communicate ideas and information by visual means *on paper*. But in everyday life, we all make use of non-verbal communication. This means communication without using words.

Non-verbal communication may be by signs. These can be facial — a yawn, a smile, a frown, putting your tongue out, and so on. They can be with the hand — the clenched fist, a handshake, or a wave of the arm. They can also be in the way you sit or stand. None of these methods involves the use of words.

Non-verbal messages can also be passed on by *sounds* — think of a baby gurgling and crying. And, when they do speak, people are still communicating non-verbally — that is, by the tone of their voice and by laughing, whispering, shouting.

All of these techniques of communication are effective in one way or another in getting the message across.

At work, too, non-verbal communication is important, and you should be able to recognise the message behind the sounds, the gestures. Let's examine some of them.

Match the signs and facial expressions to the meanings given below.

- Just watch it, mate!
- Good luck!
- That's right!
- I'm bored!
- Oh no — disaster!
- Spot on!
- You'll be alright with me!
- Turn it down!

Make a list of the ways in which we communicate by gesture or by using our bodies. You could start with a handshake and a wink. Say what message each gesture is trying to put across, such as:
- a firm handshake — I am a reliable and trustworthy person who isn't at all nervous;
- a crushing handshake — I am a tough character, so don't pick a quarrel with me!

Dressing for the part

Another way in which we communicate without words is by what we wear. People show their personalities in their clothes, as you will have noticed when walking around the shops or watching people in the street or at a concert.

At work, there may be strict rules about what you have to wear. Examples are nurses, the police, miners, traffic wardens, and so on. For jobs like these and many others, there may be a uniform. In a factory, you may have to put on overalls, special shoes or boots, helmets, or other forms of protection. You have to wear these clothes for a good reason — usually it's a question of health or safety — and the management will explain the rules to you when you start work.

All the same, it's amazing how people manage to reveal something of themselves even when they are in a standard uniform. It may be the way a hat is tilted, or a brooch in an overall, the use of make-up, and a hundred and one other ways.

You will be told what kind of clothes to wear when you attend the interview or shortly before you start the job. There may be no restrictions or advice at all. When you do start a job, notice the kind of clothes that people wear — even though they may be unaware of it, people are giving clues to themselves in their choice of tie, blouse, rings, the use of cosmetics, shoes, and in many other different ways.

Let's take an example. The drawing below shows four young people waiting to be interviewed for a job. It's an office job — assistant to the floor manager in an electrical shop selling radios, video

recorders, televisions, etc. With a friend, discuss who you think will (and will not) get the job. Give your reasons.

Visual media

'Visual media' is a phrase used for forms of communication where the message is carried by pictures. This can be done in various ways. Here are some of them:

- photographs,
- television,
- computers,
- films,
- videos.

Can you think of any other ways? Some of them have already been described in Chapter 3, on Looking. They involve a match of pictures and print. In visual media, it is the pictures which tell the story, and sometimes there is no accompanying print at all (and in the case of silent films, no sound either).

You see plenty of evidence of the effectiveness of visual media. For example, one of the most effective sales techniques is by television advertisements. We all have our favourites: yours may be one of the car adverts, or one for a beer ('refreshes the parts other beers cannot reach'), chocolate, or another product. Television directors and designers show great skill in thinking up and producing adverts which catch people's

attention. Why do they do it? Why do big companies (and small ones, too) spend tens of thousands of pounds on a single advert on TV?

The answer is *response*. You'll remember that response is one of the important aspects of communication. The aim is to trigger a reaction — to get the viewer, the customer, thinking 'That sounds good' or 'I'll ask for that one the next time I'm in the shop.'

The skilful advertiser on TV is trying to do more than that, though. The objective is to impress the name of the product — Guinness, Heineken, Stone's, Double Diamond — on your mind, so that the next time you go into a bar and the barman says 'What'll you have?', you immediately respond 'Oh, I'll have a . . . .' Bingo! The ad people have persuaded you to buy through a kind of automatic response.

Video is another effective way of getting a message across. Think of the videos which illustrate the latest pop record in the charts. They are very skilfully made, linking music, words, and moving pictures in a dramatic way. There are two objectives here: one is to entertain, but the second is the same as an advert — to get you to buy the record or cassettte.

Making a video

The crew in the photograph below is making a video with a group of children. What's going on? There are five members of the crew in the picture. They all have different jobs to do. By studying the picture, work out what the five jobs are.

Photography

At work, it will be unusual if video, television, or film are used as part of your everyday job (unless you are making them!). But photographs are used all the time, in many different ways. Let's make a list of them:

- advertising,
- press releases,
- technical books,
- identity cards,
- sports teams,
- job applications,
- company brochures,
- social events,
- safety notices.

Can you think of any others?

Of all these, the biggest use of photographs is in advertising. If you look through any newspaper or magazine, you'll see dozens of brilliant photographs. We are all so accustomed to seeing outstanding photographs that we don't always realise how skilful the photographer has been. But if your company or organisation is trying to sell its products or its services, superb photographs are essential.

Let's look at just one. Because of the expanding computing business, every company has to try harder to sell its computers or office systems. In the advert below, the photographer (working with a graphic designer) has made an eye-catching image.

Look at the advert and read the text. Then analyse it:

- What is the message?
- Who is the sender? Who is the receiver?
- Are the photographs and the design effective? If so, how?
- Effect — if you were an office manager looking to automate the office, would you buy?

WHEN YOU'RE A GENERATION AHEAD, YOU WON'T BE A PRISONER OF YOUR IN-TRAY.

DATA GENERAL INTEGRATED OFFICE AUTOMATION.

When there's a vital decision to be made, the last place the relevant information should be buried is beneath a ton of mail in your in-tray.

ELECTRONIC MAIL.

With Data General's CEO® Comprehensive Electronic Office, information is delivered electronically. Instantly. And accurately.

It includes a "certified mail" feature similar to Registered Mail that lets you confirm that communications have been seen by the intended party. And an "urgent" signal that flags important messages. But that's only the beginning.

TOTAL OFFICE AUTOMATION.

The CEO® system automates just about everything in your office. CEO® electronic filing works the way you do. Its electronic calendar keeps tabs on trips, appointments and meetings – even confirming them all.

Of course, CEO® includes easy-to-use word processing. And everything is integrated with data processing for total decision support.

CEO® even has an exclusive button that lets you handle typical interruptions. And then returns automatically to where you left off.

DON'T THROW-AWAY YOUR EXISTING EQUIPMENT.

Best of all, instead of having to throw out your existing equipment to automate your office, you can build the CEO system around it. Because it not only ties in with other Data General computers, but also ties in with the most widely-used mainframe and word processor.

Instead of having just a series of personal computers, each CEO work station becomes part of a global network, with access to data from IBM mainframes.

So it really protects your investment!

ALL FOR LESS THAN £4,000 PER WORKSTATION.

Data General's CEO system brings you all these benefits for less than £4,000 per user, depending on application. Find out more, complete the coupon today.

Data General Limited, Trident House, Renfrew Road, Paisley, PA3 4EF. Tel: 041 889 1631. I'd like all the facts on CEO – the system that makes you a generation ahead.

Name _____
Position _____
Company _____
Address _____
_____
Telephone _____

◖Data General
a Generation ahead.

SB11/9

CEO is a registered trademark of Data General. Copyright © 1983 Data General Corporation. Westboro. USA

Computers and electronic communication

Today, almost every employee and trainee is expected to know something about computers and computing.

This isn't the book to teach you about computing — you need a special course and different books to do that job. But you will already have seen that computers are vitally important for communication. They *store* information. They *process* and *display* information. And, beyond these impressive capabilities, computers can *transmit* or pass on information (data) by electronic means, controlled by an operator. They are therefore very important for communication, either in a computer room or between company branches in many towns and many countries.

Furthermore, through advanced electronic methods of communication, messages can be passed across the world in seconds. Telecommunications, the use of robots, the mixture of computers and video to make what is called 'interactive video' (where the user can be taught through a video and practises the skills or works out answers on a computer) are with us now. You may come across these methods of communication in your company.

If you don't get involved in advanced systems, you are bound to see (and use) desk-top computers, the telephone, perhaps the telex, and all kinds of electronic controls on machinery. In this way, you will come into contact with modern forms of communication. We need another book to explain how these systems work, and as you proceed with your work and training you will probably find out more about them. For the moment, all you have to know is that they are very powerful means of communication.

But, in the end, all the systems (even the robots) are designed for the objectives we set right back at the beginning of this book:

sender →message →receiver →response

On your work-experience project, or as part of your college course or your work in a company or organisation, write a report on the modern methods of electronic communication used there. Start with the telephone. The list should become quite extensive. Illustrate it with photographs, pictures, or drawings — perhaps cut from magazines, brochures, or newspapers. Remember that you are communicating, too, so design the project, making a workbook or project-book out of it. Remember all the time that *you* are communicating a message, and that all the four elements of successful communication should be in it.